Learning English

Orange Line 1

Unterrichtswerk für Orientierungsstufen, Förderstufen, Gesamtschulen und andere differenzierende Schulformen

Herausgegeben von
Werner Beile, Alice Beile-Bowes
und Helmut Reisener

sowie Manfred Bojes, Ekhard Ninnemann, Michael Plaumann, Elmar Tegethoff und Rolf-G. Wiele

unter Mitwirkung und Leitung der Verlagsredaktion Neue Sprachen

Ernst Klett Verlag

Learning English – Orange Line 1
für Klasse 5 an Orientierungsstufen, Förderstufen, Gesamtschulen
und anderen differenzierenden Schulformen

Herausgegeben von

Dr. Werner Beile und Alice Beile-Bowes M.A., Wuppertal;
Dr. Helmut Reisener, Lüneburg

sowie Manfred Bojes, Lohne; Ekhard Ninnemann, Lüneburg; Michael Plaumann, Friedberg;
Elmar Tegethoff, Hannover; Rolf-G. Wiele, Rinteln

unter Mitwirkung und Leitung

der Verlagsredaktion Neue Sprachen; Mitarbeit an diesem Werk:
Dr. Volkhart Weizsäcker, Redaktionsleiter;
Peter Cole M.A., Heinz-Peter Gerlinger, Verlagsredakteure

Visuelle Gestaltung:
Wolfgang Metzger, Mühlacker

Sprachcassetten

Zur Verbesserung der Aussprache empfiehlt es sich, die Begleitcassetten zu diesem Lehrwerk zu verwenden.

- *1 Compact-Cassette* für den Schüler mit Lektionstexten, Gedichten und Liedern. Beide Seiten besprochen. Klettnummer 58717.
  Lieferung durch jede Buchhandlung oder, wo dies auf Schwierigkeiten stößt, zuzüglich Portokosten per Nachnahme vom Ernst Klett Verlag, Postfach 1170, 7054 Korb.

- *1 Compact-Cassette* für den Lehrer mit Hörverstehenstexten, den Ausspracheübungen, den Rollenspielen und Versprachlichung der Bildgeschichten. Beide Seiten besprochen. Klettnummer 58718.
  Lieferung direkt an Lehrer, Schulstempel erforderlich.

ISBN 3-12-587110-7

1. Auflage   1 7 6 5 4 3 | 1990 89 88 87 86

Alle Drucke dieser Auflage können im Unterricht nebeneinander benutzt werden, sie sind untereinander unverändert. Die letzte Zahl bezeichnet das Jahr dieses Druckes.
© Ernst Klett Verlage GmbH u. Co. KG, Stuttgart 1984. Alle Rechte vorbehalten.
Umschlag: Gebhardt und Lorenz, Korntal.
Druck: Ernst Klett Druckerei. Printed in Germany.

Inhaltsverzeichnis

Unit/Steps	*Sprechabsichten/Themen	Strukturen	Seite

rst Scenes

York — 7

1	Good morning	– Sich begrüßen und vorstellen – Den Namen einer Person erfragen	– *What is your name?* – *my, your; I'm*	8
2	Kevin	– Etwas richtigstellen – Sich entschuldigen – Sich bedanken	– *I'm not ...* – *you are/are you?*	9
3	Sorry, no idea	– Unwissen ausdrücken	– *he, she; his, her* – *he is/is he?*	10
4	The new boy	– Fragen, wo sich etwas/jemand befindet – Informationen über sich und andere geben	– *Where is ...? It's/I'm here.* – short forms *he's, she's, you're*	11
5	Selby Road	– Besitzverhältnisse ausdrücken – Angaben zur Familie machen	– s-genitive with names – *Is that ...? That is* – *we, our*	14
6	The Pearsons	– Auskunft über Personen geben	– *isn't, aren't;* questions and short answers with *to be* – *they, their*	17
7	The new shop	– Besitz ausdrücken – Dinge und Personen beschreiben	– *has/hasn't got;* short answers with *has/hasn't* – prepositions	20
8	Ronny	– zusammenhängende Angaben über Personen machen	– *have got;* short answers with *have/haven't; there is* – questions with *who*	23
9	Timmy	– Einen Tagesablauf beschreiben – Ein Telefongespräch führen	– adverbials Grammar §§ 1–10	26

1	Barbara	– Kontakt aufnehmen und sich vorstellen – Herkunft erfragen	– *there is; that is* – short forms of *to be* – *Where is it from?*	28
2	Can you speak English?	– Fähigkeiten erfragen – Widersprechen	– *can/can't*	31
3	Let's test Barbara's English	– Im Unterrichtsgespräch fragen, antworten, berichten, bestätigen	– *What's this in English? What about ...?* – *this/that* – mixed question forms; short answers	33

⟨Authentic Britain: At the newsagent's⟩ — 35

Grammar §§ 11–13

---

* Es werden bei jeder Lektion nur die wichtigsten kommunikativen Ziele der Texte bzw. der Übungen aufgeführt. Eine vollständige Übersicht über die Lernziele und ihre Wiederholung gibt das Lehrerbuch (Klettnummer 58713).

Unit/Steps	*Sprechabsichten/Themen	Strukturen	Seite
2 ⟨Photo page: Work and play⟩			36
1 One, two, three	– Zahlenangaben machen – Telefonnummern angeben	– cardinal numbers 1–12 – regular plurals; *How many...?* – *there's/there are*	37
2 Can I help?	– Hilfe anbieten und erbitten – Um Erlaubnis fragen	– *can/can't*	39
3 Saturday morning	– Vorgänge ausdrücken, die gerade geschehen – Ortsangaben machen	– present progressive (affirmative, negative and interrogative, with *who* and *what*)	40
4 12 o'clock	– Vorgänge ausdrücken, die gerade geschehen	– present progressive	42
What are they doing?			45
		Grammar §§ 14–15	
3 ⟨Photo page: British school children⟩			46
1 School uniform	– Verpflichtung und Erlaubnis ausdrücken – Farbangaben machen – Über Kleidung sprechen	– Revision: *can/can't* – *must* – *What colour is...?*	47
2 Homework	– Sich gegenseitig Hilfe/Lösungen anbieten	– *a/an; the* [ðə/ði:]	49
3 Behind the door	– Vorschläge machen – Etwas begründen – Überraschung ausdrücken – Vorgänge ausdrücken, die gerade geschehen	– s-genitive – *why, because* Revision: present progressive, short answers, *can/can't*, questions with *what*	51
The Alphabet			56
⟨Authentic Britain: Signs⟩			57
		Grammar §§ 16–19	
4 1 Tangram Puzzles	– Gegenstände benennen – Tätigkeiten beschreiben	– *these/those* – plurals with *-es*; irregular plurals	58
2 Over and out	– Ein Taxi bestellen – Eine Adresse erfragen – Falsche Aussagen richtigstellen	– object pronouns – imperatives: *Come in, please.*	60
⟨Authentic Britain: Taxi!⟩			61
3 The box in the attic	– Anweisungen geben	– short form of *has got* – Revision: *can/can't, must, have got;* object pronouns; present progressive	63
		Grammar §§ 20–24	

Unit/Steps	*Sprechabsichten/Themen	Strukturen	Seite

5

⟨Photo page: At the breakfast table⟩ — 68

1 Numbers	– Zahlenangaben machen	– cardinal numbers 12–200	69
2 The bus driver	– Vorgänge ausdrücken, die immer wieder geschehen – Zeitangaben machen	– simple present, habitual function – adverbials – telling the time: 5 o'clock, quarter to (past), half past	70
3 Kate's kite	– Aufeinanderfolgende Handlungen schildern	– simple present, narrative usage – simple present, irregular forms	73
4 Bonzo the dog	– Vorgänge ausdrücken, die immer wieder geschehen, und aufeinanderfolgende Handlungen schildern	– simple present, habitual and narrative functions; simple present plus adverb of frequency – word order Grammar §§ 25–31	75

6

⟨Photo page: Whitby⟩ — 80

1 By train to Whitby	– Wünsche äußern	– contrast of present progressive and simple present – *want to* – *who* as subject	81
2 Picnic food	– bitten, anbieten, annehmen, ablehnen – Essen	– *have a* partitive *of* – Revision: imperatives	83
3 Seaside Special	– Ein Erlebnis erzählen – Über das Wetter sprechen – Eine Bitte äußern – Freude ausdrücken	– Revision: contrast of present progressive and present simple	85

⟨Authentic Britain: Moorsrail⟩ — 90

Grammar §§ 32–33

7

⟨Photo page: Houses in Britain⟩ — 91

1 The 'Twenty Questions' game	– Fragen stellen und kurz beantworten – verneinen	– questions with *do*; negative statements with *don't*; short answers with *do* and *don't*	92
2 All about Kevin	– Über das Frühstück sprechen	– *wh*-questions with *do*	94
3 Upstairs and Downstairs	– Spielregeln erfragen und erklären – Nichtverstehen ausdrücken	– questions with *does*; negative statements with *doesn't*; short answers with *does* and *doesn't* Grammar §§ 34–37	96

Fun pages	100
Additum zu Unit 5	106
Additum zu Unit 6	110
Additum zu Unit 7	115

Das Additum enthält weiterführende Übungen und Texte zu den jeweils genannten Units.

Grammar	119
Verzeichnis der grammatischen Ausdrücke	119
Register des Grammatikanhangs	140
Vocabulary	141
Alphabetical word list	168
⟨**Useful phrases in class**⟩	180

Die Texte, auf die sich die Hörverstehensaufgaben beziehen, sind auf der Lehrercassette (Klettnummer 58718) und im Lehrerbuch (Klettnummer 58713) verfügbar.

Zeichenerklärung

    Hörverstehensaufgaben

⟨ ⟩   Stücke in Winkelklammern sind fakultativ.

   Das Stück ist auf der Cassette für Schüler und Lehrer (Klettnummer 58717) verfügbar.

   Das Stück ist auf der Cassette für Lehrer (Klettnummer 58718) verfügbar.

    Übungen, die die Schüler auffordern, über sich und ihre eigene Situation innerhalb und außerhalb des Klassenzimmers zu sprechen.

    Grammar box

First Scenes

York

First Scenes

1 Good morning

a) *Teacher:* Good morning.
I'm your teacher.
My name is Mrs Griffin.

b) *Ronny:* Hello.
New boy: Hello.
Ronny: What is your name?
New boy: Kevin.
Ronny: My name is Ronny.
Ronny Bennett.

Dialogues

1 "Hello, I'm David."
"I'm Jane. Hello, David."

2 "What is your name?"
"My name is Jane."

3 "My name is…
What is your name?"

4 OVER TO YOU

David / Jane

Jim / John

Helen / Jenny

Penny / Tony

First Scenes

2 Kevin

a) *Teacher:* Good morning, Jane.
   Helen: I'm not Jane.
   I'm Helen.
   Teacher: Oh, sorry, Helen.

b) *Teacher:* Are you new?
   Kevin: Yes.
   Teacher: What is your name?
   Kevin: Kevin Pearson.
   Teacher: You are in 1B, Kevin.
   Kevin: Thank you.

Dialogues

1 "Hello, Penny."
  "I'm not Penny.
  I'm Jane."
  "Oh, sorry, Jane."

2 "Is your name Penny?"
  "No, my name is Jenny."

3 "Are you Jim?"
  "No, I'm John."

4 "Are you { new?"   "Yes/no."
            in 1B?"
            David?"

Look, listen and say

[dʒ] **J**im, **J**ohn, **J**enny, **J**ane.   Are you **J**enny? – No, I'm **J**ane.

[e]   H**e**len, K**e**vin, P**e**nny, J**e**nny.   H**e**llo, P**e**nny.

nine

First Scenes

3 Sorry, no idea

a) *Ronny:* Look at that boy. He is new.
   Girl: Is he in 1A?
   Ronny: No, he is in 1B.
   Girl: What is his name?
   Ronny: His name is Kevin.

b) *Helen:* Look at that teacher. Is she new?
   Ronny: Yes, she is the new English teacher.
   Kevin: What is her name?
   Helen: Sorry, no idea.

Dialogues

1. "Look at that boy. He is new."
   "Look at that girl. She … ."
2. "Is his name Ben?"
      "No, his name is Kevin."
   "Is her name Ann?"
      "No, … Helen."
   (Ronny? Penny? Kevin? Jane?)
3. "Sorry, what is his/her name?"
   "His/her name is … ."
4. "Is he/she in 1A?"
   "No, he/she is in 1B."

5. "Look at that … Is she new?"
   "…"
   "Is her name Mrs Bennett?"
   …
   "Sorry, what is her name?"
   …
   "Is she the new … teacher?"
   …

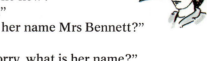

First Scenes

4 The new boy

a) *Teacher:* Good morning, boys and girls.
I'm Mrs Griffin.
I'm your English teacher.
Boys and girls: Good morning, Mrs Griffin.

b) *Mrs Griffin:* Where is the register?
Boy: It's here.
Mrs Griffin: Thank you. – Helen Barnes?
Helen: Here.
Mrs Griffin: Ronny Bennett?
Ronny: Here.
Mrs Griffin: Christine Cook? Where is Christine Cook?
Girl: She's ill.

c) *Mrs Griffin:* Ben MacDonald?
Where is Ben?
He's late.
Ben: I'm here.
Mrs Griffin: You're late, Ben.
Ben: I'm sorry.

d) *Mrs Griffin:* Where is the new boy?
Kevin: I'm here.
Mrs Griffin: What is your name, please?
Kevin: Kevin Pearson.
Mrs Griffin: Where are you from?
Kevin: I'm from Leeds.

eleven

First Scenes

1 Questions and answers

Where is | Christine / the new boy / the new girl / the new teacher / the register / Helen / Ben / …

He's / She's / It's | here.

2 Find the right words

a) 1. I **am** new. → **I'm** new.
   2. You … ill. → **You're** ill.
   3. He … the new boy. → … the new boy.
   4. She … late. → …
   5. I … not Jane. → …
   6. You … in 1A. → …
   7. He … in 1B. → …

b) 1. Mrs Griffin **is** the new teacher.
      → She's the new teacher.
   2. Christine … ill. → … ill.
   3. Kevin … from Leeds. → …
   4. The register … here. → …
   5. Ben … in 1B. → …
   6. The word … new. → …

```
I'm    –  I am
you're –  you are
he's   –  he is
she's  –  she is
it's   –  it is
```

3 I, my; you, your; he, his; she, her; it.

a) 1. Where is Christine Cook?
      …'s ill.

   2. …'re late, Ben!
      Sorry …'m late.

   3. Look at that boy.
      …'s new.

   4. Where is the register?
      …'s here.

b) 1. What is your name?
      … name is Penny.

   2. Look at that girl.
      What is … name?

   3. I'm Mrs Griffin.
      I'm … new teacher.

   4. Look at that boy.
      What is … name?

c) 1. Are you English?
      No, …'m not English.
      … name is Karsten.

   2. That girl is in 1B.
      … name is Jenny.
      …'s English.

   3. Kevin is new.
      …'s in 1B.
      Mrs Griffin is … teacher.

   4. Hello. Are … new?
      What is … name?

First Scenes

4 Make questions

Example: (I am late) → Am I late?

1. *(He is new) → …*
2. *(You are ill) → …*
3. *(She is from Leeds) → …*
4. *(He is the new boy) → …*
5. *(You are in 1 B) → …*
6. *(Mrs Griffin is the new teacher) → …*
7. *(Ronny is from York) → …*
8. *(Mrs Pearson is late) → …*
9. *(Ben is late) → …*
10. *(You are from York) → …*

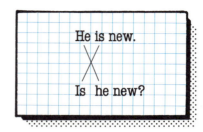

5 What is his answer?

a) It's here.
b) Sorry I'm late.
c) I'm from Leeds.
d) Good morning.
e) I'm here.
f) I'm not Andy. I'm Kevin.
g) My name is Kevin Pearson.

6 What is his question?

a)

1. "No, I'm not in 1B. I'm in 1A."
2. "No, I'm not Penny. I'm Jenny."
3. "I'm from York."
4. "The register? It's here."
5. "No. Not Mrs Bennett.
   Her name is Mrs Griffin."

b) *Find the questions.*
  1. "Yes, you're late."
  2. "Jenny is here."
  3. "My name is Tom."
  4. "He's from York."
  5. "No, I'm not Kevin. I'm Andy."

thirteen 13

First Scenes

5 Selby Road

a) *Ronny:* Where is your new house?
Kevin: It's a flat, not a house.
It's in Selby Road.
Ronny: We're in Selby Road, too.
Kevin: Good.

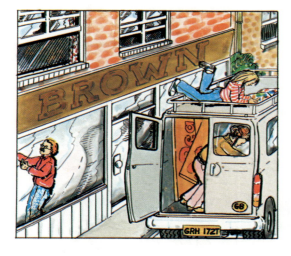

b) *Kevin:* Look, that is our new flat.
And that is our new shop.
Ronny: Is that your father in the shop?
Kevin: Yes, and that is my mother in the van.
Ronny: And the girl *on* the van?
Kevin: That is my sister Kate.
She's terrible.

And you're terrible, too, brother!

1 Ask your friends

1. Where is Kevin from?
2. Where is Kevin's new flat?
3. Where is Ronny's house?
4. Where is Kevin's father?
5. Where is his mother?
6. Where is his sister?

2 Find the right word – 'my' or 'our'?

1. *Kevin:* "That is … sister."
2. *Kevin and Kate:* "That is … flat."
3. *Kevin:* "That is … friend Ronny."
4. *Ronny and Kevin:* "That is … teacher."
5. *Kate:* "That is … mother."
6. *Mr and Mrs Pearson:* "That is … shop."
7. *Ronny and Kevin:* "That is … road."
8. *Kevin:* "That is … father."

3 Look, listen and say

[eɪ] David
name
say
late

Hello, is your n**a**me Kate?
No, my n**a**me is J**a**ne.

14 *fourteen*

First Scenes

fifteen

First Scenes

4 Selby Road

Example: 1. **Kevin's flat** is in Selby Road.
            2. ... is in Selby Road, too.
3. Mr Pearson is ...
4. Mrs Pearson is ...
5. ... is terrible.
6. Ronny is ...

5 We're here

Examples: "Kevin and Ronny, where are you?"
             "We're in the van."
             "Ronny, where are you?"
             "I'm in the shop."

we're – we are

6 Make questions and ask your friends

Example:

"Where is Kevin's friend?"
"He's in the flat."
"Where is ...?"

First Scenes

6 The Pearsons

a) *Mr Pearson:* Where is Kate?
She isn't in the flat.
And she isn't in the shop.
Is she in the van?
Mrs Pearson: No, she isn't.
Kevin: Look, Mum, *on* the van!
Mrs Pearson: *On* the van?
Oh, Kate!

b)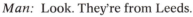

Man: Look. They're from Leeds.
That is their van.
Their name is Pearson.

c)

Woman: Are they new in Selby Road?
Man: Yes, they are.
Woman: Are they from York?
Man: No, they aren't.
Woman: Where are they from?
Man: They're from Leeds.
Woman: Is that their van?
Man: Yes, it is.
Woman: Brown – is that their name?
Man: No, it isn't.
Their name is Pearson.

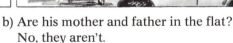

they're – they are
isn't – is not
aren't – are not

1 Yes, he is – no, he isn't

a) Is Kevin in the flat?   No, he isn't.
Is he in the shop?   …
Is he in the van?   Yes, he is.
Is he in York?   …
Is he in Leeds?   …

b) Are his mother and father in the flat?
No, they aren't.
Are they in the shop? …
Are they in the van? Yes, they are.
Are they in York? …
Are they in Leeds? …

c) Kate?
…

d) the Pearsons?
…

seventeen 17

First Scenes

2 Answer the questions

Examples: Are the Pearsons new in Selby Road? – Yes, they are.
Is Ronny new in Selby Road? – No, he isn't.

1. Is Mrs Pearson Kevin's mother?
2. Is Kate Ronny's sister?
3. Is Ronny from York?
4. Are the Pearsons from York?
5. Is the new shop in Leeds?
6. Is the new shop in Selby Road?
7. Are Kevin and Kate brother and sister?
8. Are Kevin and Ronny in 1A?
9. Is Mrs Griffin their English teacher?
10. Are Kevin and Kate Ronny's new friends?

3 Where are they?

Where is / Where are

Ronny / you / the register / the Pearsons ...

?

She's / We're / He's / The Pearsons ... / It's / They're / are

in Leeds. / in the shop. / in the van. / in York. / here. / in the flat.

4 Look, is that Mrs Griffin?

Examples:

Is **that** Mrs Griffin? – Yes, **it** is.
Is **that** our register? – No, **it** isn't.

… Helen's father? …
… Ronny's house? …
… Kevin's van? …
… the new shop? …
… Kate? …

5 Kate

Girl: Are you the new girl?	*Kate:* Yes, I am.
Girl: Are you Kate Bennett?	*Kate?* No, …
	… Kate Pearson.
Girl: Are you Kevin's sister?	*Kate:* …
Girl: Are you new in Selby Road?	*Kate:* …
Girl: Are you from York?	*Kate:* …
	… from Leeds.

First Scenes

6 Find the right words

1. I'm Kate. **My** brother is Kevin.
2. That is Mr Pearson. … van is in Selby Road.
3. Kate's mother is in the shop. …name is Mrs Pearson.
4. They aren't the Browns. …name is Pearson.
5. You're new. What is …name?
6. We're new in Selby Road. That is … shop.
7. I'm your teacher. … name is Mrs Griffin.

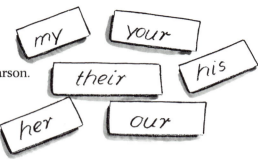

1. I'm the new teacher. — **My** name is Mrs Griffin.
   You're late. — What is **your** name?
   He's ill. — **His** name is Kevin.
   She's ill, too. — What is **her** name?
   We're from Leeds. — That is **our** flat.
   Hello, Kevin. Hello, Kate.
   You're new. — Where is **your** new house?
   They're in the shop. — **Their** flat is in Selby Road.

2. Are **you** the new girl? — Yes, **I** am. / No, **I**'m not.
   Is **Kevin** late? — Yes, **he** is. / No, **he** isn't.
   Is **Kate** terrible? — Yes, **she** is. / No, **she** isn't.
   Is **the new shop** in Selby Road? — Yes, **it** is. / No, **it** isn't.
   Is **that** the new teacher? — Yes, **it** is. / No, **it** isn't.
   Is **that** your house? — Yes, **it** is. / No, **it** isn't.
   Are **you** from York? — Yes, **we** are. / No, **we** aren't.
   Are **they** in the flat? — Yes, **they** are. / No, **they** aren't.

7 Look, listen and say

[æ]
That is **A**nn's flat.
That is **D**an's v**a**n.
Are you in the v**a**n, **D**an?

[e]
H**e**len is K**e**vin's fri**e**nd.
Yes, B**e**n is in
S**e**lby Road.

[ð]
Tha**t** is **th**eir fa**th**er.
Tha**t** is **th**eir mo**th**er.
They are in **th**e shop.

[æ] - [e]
K**e**vin is in the v**a**n
in S**e**lby Road.
Dan and B**e**n are terrible.
Are you in K**e**vin's fl**a**t?
Yes, I **a**m.

nineteen 19

First Scenes

7 The new shop

a) The new shop is dirty.
Look at the floor!
The window is dirty!
The door and the cupboard
are dirty, too.
Is the chair clean?
No, it isn't. It is dirty, too.

b) Here is Mrs Pearson.
She has got a box under her arm.
She has got a sponge, too.
And here is Mr Pearson.
He hasn't got a box and a sponge.
But he has got a bucket and a brush.
He has got water in the bucket.

1 Yes, it is/No, it isn't

Examples:
Is the window dirty? – Yes, it is.
Is the floor clean? – No, it isn't.

1. Is the shop clean?
2. Is the shop dirty?
3. Is the window clean?
4. Is the door dirty?
5. Is the chair clean?
6. Is the cupboard clean?

2 Mr and Mrs Pearson

What has Mrs Pearson got?
What has Mr Pearson got?

3 Yes, he has/No, he hasn't

Examples:
Has Mr Pearson got a bucket? – Yes, he has.
Has Mrs Pearson got a bucket? – No, she hasn't.

1. Has Mr Pearson got a brush?
2. Has Mrs Pearson got a sponge?
3. Has Mr Pearson got a sponge?
4. Has Mrs Pearson got a brush?
5. Has Mr Pearson got a box?
6. Has Mrs Pearson got a box?

c) The shop is clean now. The brush is behind the door. The box is on the chair. And the water in the bucket is dirty now. Kevin and Kate are in front of the shop.

Mr Pearson: What has Kevin got? Is it a water-pistol?

Mrs Pearson: No, no. He hasn't got a water-pistol.
Mr Pearson: Yes, he has.
Mrs Pearson: No, he hasn't. Come on.

But Kevin *has* got a water-pistol. It is new. Oh dear!

4 Look at the shop now!

Example: The brush is in the cupboard.

5 Oh dear!

a) Kevin hasn't got a water-pistol now. He has got a … And Kate …

b) *Make questions.*

Has got a  ? Yes,/No, he/she has./hasn't.

6 Where are they?

Make questions and answers.

a) Where is Ronny? — He's …
   …   Kate? — She's …
   …   the bucket? — It's …
b) Is Ronny in front of the van? — No, he isn't.
   … Kevin …   …? — …   …
c) Has Ronny got a water-pistol? — No, he hasn't.
   … Kate …   bucket? — … she …
d) Is the van clean? — No, it isn't.
   Is the van dirty? — Yes, it is.
   …   door …? — No, it isn't.
   …   window …? — No idea.

7 Mrs Pearson and her shop

1. Is Mrs Pearson from Leeds?
2. Has she got a flat in Selby Road?
3. Is she Ronny's mother?
4. Has Kevin got a brother?
5. Is Kate Kevin's sister?
6. Has the shop got a cupboard?
7. Is the shop dirty now?
8. Has the cupboard got a door?
9. Is Mrs Pearson a teacher?
10. Has Mr Pearson got a van?

8 Look, listen and say

[r] Ronny's brother isn't terrible.
     Is Christine Ronny's friend?
     Ronny's father is in front of his taxi.

[ʌ] My brother has got a bucket.
     The sponge is in the cupboard.
     The brush is in front of the door.

First Scenes

8 Ronny

a) *Ronny:* Mum, I have got a new friend.
His name is Kevin Pearson.
He has got a sister.
His parents have got a shop.
Look, that is their shop.
It has got a new name now.
Mother: Oh yes, Pearson.

b) *Kevin:* Who is that?
Ronny: My baby brother Timmy.
Kevin: You have got a baby brother!
Ronny: Yes.
Kevin: That is terrible.
Ronny: Oh no, it isn't!
It's great!

c) That is Ronny's house.
The house next door is empty.
There is a taxi in front of Ronny's house.
It is his mother's taxi.
The Bennetts have got two taxis.
Ronny's father is a taxi driver.
And his mother is a taxi driver, too.

First Scenes

1 Answer the questions

Has Ronny got a brother?
Has Kevin got a brother?
Have Ronny's parents got a shop?
Have Kevin's parents got a van?
Has Kate got a brother?
Has the shop got a new name?
Have Ronny's parents got a flat?
Have his parents got a van?
Have they got a cat?

Yes, he/she/it has.
No, he/she/it hasn't.
Yes, they have.
No, they haven't.

hasn't – has not
haven't – have not

2 Who is that?

Who is that? – That is Ronny. He's Kevin's friend.
He's Timmy's brother
– That is Kevin. He's Kate's …
…

3 My new friend

Kevin:
Mum, I have got a new friend.
His name is …
His father is …
and his mother is …
He hasn't got a sister, he …

4 Make it right

Example: The Bennetts have got a flat. –
The Bennetts haven't got a flat. They have got a house.

1. The Pearsons have got a house.
2. Kevin has got a baby brother.
3. Kate has got a sister.
4. Ronny's parents have got a van.
5. The Pearsons have got two boys.
6. Kevin's parents have got two taxis.
7. The Bennetts have got two girls.
8. Ronny has got a baby sister.
9. The Pearsons have got a shop in Leeds.
10. Timmy has got a water-pistol.

First Scenes

5 There is – there isn't

a) 1. There is a box on the floor. 2. There is a … 3. …

b) 1. Is there a bucket on the floor? – No, there isn't.
   Is there a box on the floor? – Yes, there is.
   2. Is there a baby in the box?
   3. Is there a taxi in front of the shop?
   4. Is there a taxi behind the house?
   5. Is there a woman in the taxi?
   6. Is there a man in front of the shop?

6 Look, listen and say

[ɒ]
He has got a shop.
What is on the box?
Sorry, Don.

[ɔː]
Good morning.
Is your friend from York?
The floor and the door are dirty.

[ɒ] - [ɔː]
Tom is in York.
Your shop has got a new door.
The box on the floor is dirty.

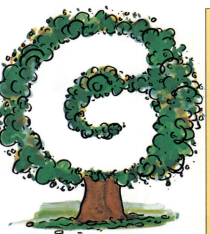

Mum, I	have got	a new friend.
You	have got	a baby brother!
He	has got	a box under his arm.
She	has got	a sponge in her bucket.
Look at the shop. It	has got	a new name now.
We	have got	a van.
You	have got	a sponge, we have got a brush.
They	have got	a new shop.
Kate	hasn't got	a sister.
The Bennetts	haven't got	a van.

Have you got a baby brother, Ronny?	Yes, I have.
Have you got a water-pistol, Ronny?	No, I haven't.
Has Kevin got a sister?	Yes, he has.
Has Mr Pearson got a taxi?	No, he hasn't.
Has Mrs Pearson got the brush?	Yes, she has.
Has Wendy got the register?	No, she hasn't.

twenty-five

First Scenes

9 Timmy

a) Timmy's parents are taxi drivers.
   In the morning   his mother   is   out in the taxi,
                       and Ronny   is   at school,
                       but his father is at home.
   In the afternoon   his father   is   out in the taxi,
                       and Ronny   is   at school,
                       but his mother is at home.
   In the evening   Ronny is at home.
   So sometimes   his father
                       and his mother are out.
   And at night?   Well, at night they are all at home, in bed.

b) Timmy has got a house.
   Well, it is not a house.
   It is a box.
   But it is Timmy's house.
   It has got two windows,
   and it has got a door.
   Timmy has got a telephone in his house.
   A toy telephone.

26 twenty-six

First Scenes

1 Is Ronny at home?

Make telephone dialogues.

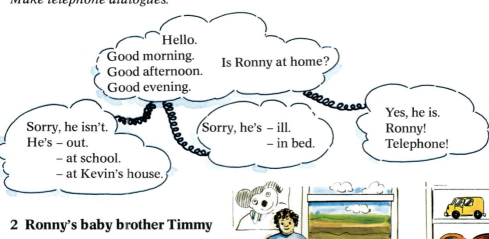

2 Ronny's baby brother Timmy

What has Timmy got?
Ask your friends.

What has Timmy got? …
Has he got a teddy? …
Where is the dog? …

Now you go on.

3 Timmy, the taxi driver

Mum: Where is Timmy?
Ronny: In his taxi.
Mum: In his what?
Ronny: In his taxi.

Say where Timmy's toys are now.

4 ⟨Let's sing a song: Hello, Timmy⟩

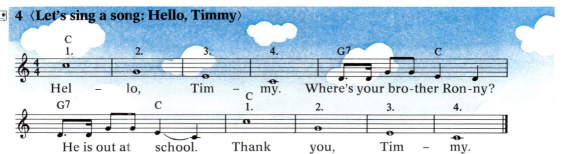

Unit 1

Unit 1 Step 1

1 Barbara

a) The house next door is empty.
Today there is a van in front of the house.

Ronny: Look, there's a van in front of the house next door.
Kevin: Where's it from?
Ronny: Köln.
Kevin: Where's that?
Ronny: No idea.
Kevin: There's a car, too.
Ronny: It hasn't got 'GB' on it, it has got 'D'.
Kevin: 'D' – that's for Denmark.
Kate: No, it isn't.
It's for Germany.
Kevin: 'D' for Germany?
Kate: 'D' for Deutschland.

b) There is a girl in the house.
She is at the window.

Ronny: Hello.
Girl: Hello.
We're new here.
Ronny: That's great.
I'm from next door.
Girl: What's your name?
Ronny: Ronny.
Kevin: My name is Kevin.
Kate: And I'm Kate.
Kevin: She's my baby sister.
Girl: I'm Barbara Klein.
Kevin: Klein? That's not English.
Barbara: No, it's German.
My father is German, and my mother is English.

Unit 1 Step 1

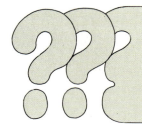

1 Answer the questions

1. What's in front of the house next door?
2. Where's it from?
3. What's behind the van?
4. What has it got on it?
5. Where's it from?
6. Who's in the house?
7. What's her name?
8. Where are her parents from?

2 Long forms and short forms

a) *What is the long form?*

1. I'm from Germany. = I am from Germany.
2. We're new here.
3. Where's your house?
4. It's in Fulford Road.
5. It isn't in Selby Road.
6. What's your name?
7. You aren't in 1 B.
8. You're in 1 A.
9. There's a car.
10. We haven't got a car.
11. We've got a van.
12. Who's in the shop?
13. That's my sister.
14. We're from York.
15. They're from Leeds.
16. They aren't from York.

b) *What is the short form?*

1. Where is Kate? = Where's Kate?
2. She is late.
3. She is not ill.
4. You are late, Kate.
5. Sorry I am late.
6. That is the new boy.
7. He is not in 1 B.
8. What is his name?
9. We are not at school today.
10. We are at home.
11. I have not got the water-pistols.
12. They are in the cupboard.
13. No, they are not in the cupboard.
14. Where is Kevin?
15. He has got the water-pistols.
16. No, he has not got the water-pistols.

c) *What is the long form? Be careful.*

1. Where's Ronny's house?
2. Mr Bennett isn't Kevin's father.
3. Kevin's father hasn't got a car.
4. Who's Ronny's friend?
5. That's Kate's brother.
6. She's Barbara's friend.

Long forms and short forms: I am → I ~~a~~m → I'm

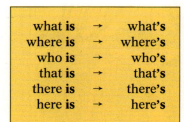

what is	→	what's
where is	→	where's
who is	→	who's
that is	→	that's
there is	→	there's
here is	→	here's

I am	→	I'm
you are	→	you're
he is	→	he's
she is	→	she's
it is	→	it's
we are	→	we're
you are	→	you're
they are	→	they're

is not	→	isn't
are not	→	aren't
have not	→	haven't
has not	→	hasn't

Unit 1 Step 2

2 Can you speak English?

a) Barbara is in the road with Kate, Ronny and Kevin.

Ronny: Where are you from in Germany?
Barbara: Köln. That's 'Cologne' in English.
Kevin: Can you speak German?
Barbara: Yes, I can.
I can speak German,
and I can speak English, too.
Kevin: You're lucky.
Have you got a brother?
Barbara: No, I haven't.
Kate: You're lucky.

b) Barbara is lucky.

She can speak German,
and she can speak English.

She can write German,
and she can write English.

She can read German books
and she can read English books.

1 Can they speak English?

a) *What about Ronny?*

    He can speak …
But he can't speak …
    He can …
But he can't …

    …

b) *What about Kevin and Kate?*

    They can …
But they can't …

c) *What about you?*

    I can …
But I can't …

d) *What about your teacher?*

2 Can Barbara speak German?

| Can | you
Ronny/he
Barbara/she
Kate and Kevin
they
we | speak
write
read | English
German
(books) | ? | Yes,

No, | I
he
she
they
we | can.

can't. |

Unit 1 Step 2

3 Mr Gossip is in the shop

a) *Mrs Pearson:*
Good morning, Mr Gossip.
Here's your newspaper.
And the magazine for Mrs Gossip.
And here's Gordon's comic.

Mr Gossip:
Thank you, Mrs Pearson. Oh, hm –
there's a new family in that empty house.
They're from Denmark.
Their name is Clean.
The father is English
and the mother is Danish.
She can't speak English.
They have got a boy.
His name is Bernard.

Kate:
That's wrong, Mr Gossip.
They're from …

Now you go on.

b) *Answer the questions.*
1. Who is in the shop?
2. Has Mr Gossip got a book?
3. What has Kate got?
4. Is Mr Gossip right or wrong?

4 Yes, she can – No, she can't

1. Can Kate read German comics?
2. Can Barbara read English comics?
3. Can Timmy write?
4. Can Kevin and Kate read English books?
5. Can the Bennetts speak German?
6. Can Ronny answer the telephone?
7. Can Timmy answer the telephone?
8. Can you read German books?

5 What's your name?

"What's your name?"
   "My name is …"
"…? That's not English."
   "No, it's German.
   My mother/father/family is …/
   My parents are …"

6 Look, listen and say

[dʒ]
Barbara is **G**erman.
She's from **G**ermany.
Jane isn't **G**erman.
What's '**r**e**g**iste**r**' in **G**erman?

[dʒ] - [tʃ]
That's our **G**erman tea**ch**er.
The **r**e**g**iste**r** is on the **ch**air.
Charlie has got a sponge.

[w]
What's dirty?
The **w**indow.
Where's the **w**ater?

32 thirty-two

Unit 1 Step 3

3 Let's test Barbara's English

a) *Ronny:* Let's play 'school'.
   Kate: Good idea.
   Let's test Barbara's English.
   O.K., Barbara?
   Barbara: Yes, O.K.
   Ronny: I'm the teacher.
   Kevin: O.K., you first,
   I'm next, then Kate.

b) *Ronny:*
   What's this in English?   *Barbara:* It's a pen.
   And this here?   It's a pencil.
   What about this?   It's a book.

   Kevin:
   What's this in English?   *Barbara:* It's a biro.
   And this?   It's a rubber.
   What about this?   It's a ruler.
   And what's the word for this? Felt pen.
   Good, Barbara.

c) *Kate:*
   What's this in English?   *Barbara:* Er … no idea.
   Look, it has got pencils
   in it.   Is it a pencil case?
   Yes, it is.

   What about this?   Er … is it a map?
   No, it isn't.
   This is a school-bag.
   That's a map over there.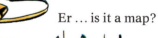

d) *Barbara:*
   And this is a magazine
   and that's a newspaper.
   Right?

   Kate:
   Right!

thirty-three 33

Unit 1 Step 3

1 Who are they?
This is Mrs Pearson and **t**hat's Mrs Bennett.

2 Test your vocabulary

This is a shop and that's a house.

This is a ... and that's ....

... ...

... ...

... ...

3 Oh no, it isn't

This is your pen.
That's my pen over there.
Go on.

Oh no, it isn't.
This is my pen.
That's your pen.

Unit 1 Step 3

⟨**Authentic Britain:
At the newsagent's**⟩

At the newsagent's you can buy things like pens, pencils, newspapers, magazines and comics. Sometimes they have got sweets, drinks and toys, too.

Unit 2

⟨Photo page: Work and play⟩

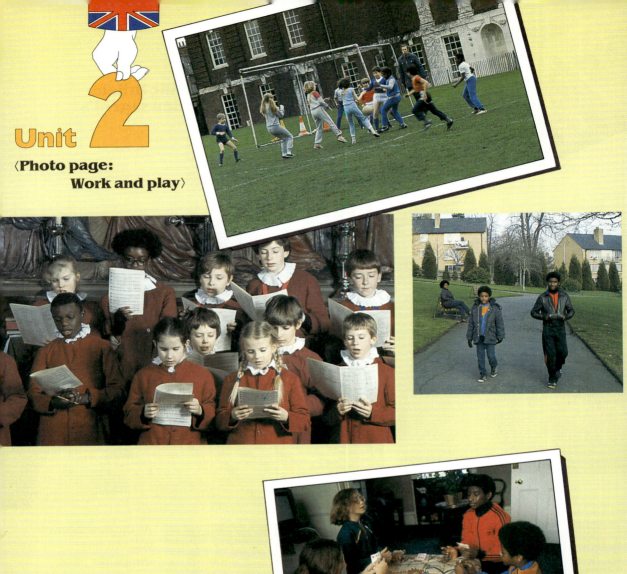

Unit 2 Step 1

1 One, two, three…

1 How old are you?

a) *Kate:* How old are you?
Barbara: I'm eleven.
 What about you?
Kate: I'm ten.
Barbara: How old is Ronny?
Kate: He's eleven.
 And Kevin is nearly twelve.
 Ronny's brother is two.
Barbara: My sister is sixteen.
Kate: You have got a sister?
Barbara: Yes, but she's still in Germany with my father.

b) *Ask your friends:* How old are you?
Where are you from?
Can you speak English?
Have you got a brother or a sister?
How old is your sister (brother, friend)?
…

2 Telephone numbers

47098 — oh
53000 23 — double oh

What's your telephone number?

3 Barbara's new friends

One, two, three, four
Bennetts in the house next door.
Kevin, parents, sister Kate,
Five, six, seven, eight.
Barbara and mother – then –
Seven, eight – nine, ten.

thirty-seven 37

Unit 2 Step 1

4 How many have they got?

[s] How many book**s** has Kevin got?
He has got two.
…   *Now you go on.*

[z] How many pen**s** has Jenny got?
She has got five.
…

5 How many are there?

| How many | pens
pencils
… | are there | in your school-bag?
on your table?
in your pencil case? |

There's one …
There are five …
…

6 A game

Kate: In my school-bag   I've got one pencil ca**s**e.
Barbara: In my school-bag   I've got one pencil ca**s**e and two rulers.
Kevin: In my school-bag   I've got one pencil ca**s**e, two rulers and three …

Unit 2 Step 2

2 Can I help?

a) *Woman:* Can you drive me to Leeds?
   Mrs Bennett: Yes, I can.

b) *Mrs Klein:* Can you run to the shop for a newspaper?
   Barbara: O.K., Mum. Can I play with Kate then?
   Mrs Klein: Yes, you can.

c) *Kevin:* Can I help you, Mum?
   Mrs Pearson: Yes, you can clean the van.
   Kate: What can I do?
   Mr Pearson: You can carry this bucket to Kevin.

d) *Mr Bennett:* Can you help me, Ronny?
   Ronny: Yes, what can I do?
   Mr Bennett: You can go for a walk with Timmy.
   Ronny: O.K. Can I wear my new pullover?
   Mr Bennett: Ask your mother.

1 Can you help me?

Make ten sentences.

	carry	the box the bucket the chair the brush	into the	shop house flat
	go for a walk with play with	… …		
Can you	clean	the taxi the car the van the shop		please?
	run to the shop for	a magazine a comic a newspaper		

Yes, I can.

No, I can't. Sorry.

thirty-nine 39

Unit 2 Step 3

3 Saturday morning

a) It is 10 o'clock on Saturday morning.
Mr Pearson is cleaning the van.
Kevin is helping his father.
Ronny is going for a walk with Timmy.
Ronny is wearing his new pullover.
Kate is playing hopscotch.
Barbara is watching.
She is sitting on the wall.
Mrs Bennett is driving her taxi.
The sun is shining.

b) Now it is 11 o'clock. It is raining.
Kevin and his father are carrying
the buckets into the shop.
And Kate and Barbara?
They are running into the house.
Ronny is running, too.
He is carrying Timmy.
Look at Timmy! Isn't he funny?
He is wearing Ronny's pullover.

1 What are they doing?

a) What is Mr Pearson doing? He is cleaning …
   What is Kate doing?   She is   … ing …
   …   Ronny …
   …   Kevin …
   …   Barbara …
   …   Mrs Bennett …

   What is Ronny wearing? …

b) What are Kevin and his father doing? They are … ing …
   …   Kate and Barbara   … ? …
   …   is Ronny   … ? He is …
   What is Timmy wearing?   …

40 *forty*

2 No, he isn't

Answer the questions.

Example: Is Mr Pearson cleaning the taxi? – No, he isn't. He is cleaning the van.
Are Kevin and his father carrying the boxes into the shop? – No, they aren't. They are ...

a) 1. Is Kevin helping his mother?
2. Is Ronny going for a walk with Kate?
3. Is Kate playing with Kevin?
4. Is Barbara sitting on a chair?
5. Is Mrs Bennett driving a taxi?

b) 1. Are Kevin and his father carrying the buckets into the flat?
2. Are Kate and Barbara running into the shop?
3. Is Ronny carrying a bucket?
4. Is Timmy wearing Kate's pullover?

3 That's wrong

Look at the pictures on page 40.
Make the sentences right.

Example: Kevin is going for a walk with Timmy.
"No, Kevin isn't going for a walk with Timmy.
He is helping his father."

a) 1. Mr Pearson is driving the van.
2. Barbara is playing hopscotch.
3. Barbara is listening.
4. Ronny is speaking to his mother.
5. It is raining.

b) 1. Kevin and his father are sitting in the van.
2. Barbara and Kate are playing with Timmy.
3. Timmy is running.
4. The sun is shining.

4 Look, listen and say

[eɪ]
You're late, David.
Her name is Jane.
Kate is playing with the baby.

[aɪ]
She is writing with my biro.
My father is a taxi driver.

[eɪ] - [aɪ]
Kate has got eight biros.
Sometimes my newspaper is late.

[w]
Where's my water-pistol?
Where are we?
What can I wear?

[v]
There are eleven vans.
I have got five pencils.
The van is very dirty.

[w] - [v]
Kevin is at the window.
Wendy is in the van.
Twelve pullovers.

Unit 2 Step 4

4 12 o'clock

Saturday morning. 12 o'clock.

Mrs Klein:
　Barbara, where are you?
Barbara:
　I'm in my room with Kate.
Mrs Klein:
　What are you doing?
Barbara:
　We're playing cards.

Mrs Pearson:
　Kevin, where are you?
Kevin:
　I'm in the shop.
Mrs Pearson:
　What are you doing?
Kevin:
　I'm reading a magazine.
Mrs Pearson:
　Well, come and
　help me.

Mrs Bennett:
　Ronny, where are you?
Ronny:
　In the bathroom.
Mrs Bennett:
　What are you doing?
Ronny:
　I'm waiting.
Mrs Bennett:
　Waiting?
Ronny:
　Yes, Timmy is sitting
　on his potty.

1 Questions

1. Where is Barbara?
2. What are Barbara and Kate doing?
3. Where is Kevin?
4. What is he doing?
5. Where are Ronny and Timmy?
6. What is Ronny doing?
7. Where is Timmy sitting?

2 Dialogues

Make dialogues.

| Barbara,
Kevin,
Kate,
Ronny, | where are you? | I'm
We're | in my room.
in Kate's room.
in the house/shop/flat.
in the car/taxi/van. |

| What are you doing? | | I'm
We're | reading a book/a magazine …
playing cards/hopscotch.
cleaning my room/my table/my school-bag …
helping my mother/my father.
watching TV. 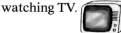 |

3 It is Saturday afternoon a) *What are they doing?*

b) *Now ask your friends.*   *Example:* 1. Look at picture 1. Is Barbara playing cards? –
                                No, she isn't playing cards. She's playing hopscotch.
2. Is Kate running into Barbara's house?   6. Are Kate and Kevin carrying buckets?
3. Is Timmy sitting on the floor?   7. Are Ronny and Timmy running?
4. Is Mr Pearson carrying Timmy?   8. Are Ronny and Kevin reading comics?
5. Are Barbara and Kate running into the shop?

4 What are you doing?

Make questions and answers.
Examples: What are you doing, Barbara? – **I**'m cleaning the window.
             What are you doing, Barbara and Ronny? – **We**'re playing cards.
Now you go on.

5 Look, listen and say

[aʊ] That's Mrs Brown's house.
Our father is out.

[əʊ] Let's go home.
Hello, let's go in.

[aʊ] - [əʊ] Our house is in Selby Road.
We have got brown pullovers.

[ð] Their mother and their father are in the shop.

[θ] Three bathrooms?
Thank you.

[ð] - [θ] Where's their bathroom?
There it is. Thank you.

a) What are you doing, Kevin?
I'm reading a magazine
and Ronny is reading a comic.
We are waiting for the girls.
They aren't playing cards,
they are playing hopscotch.

b) to wear		Timmy is	**wearing**	a pullover.
to rain		It is	**raining.**	
to drive	ℯ ing	His mother is	**driving**	the taxi.
to shine	ℯ	The sun is	**shining.**	
to sit	+t	Barbara is	**sitting**	on the wall.
to run	+n	Kate is	**running**	into the house.

6 Let's sing a song: My Bonnie is over the ocean

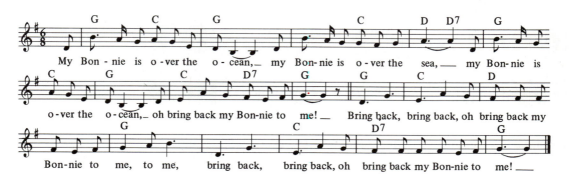

My Bon-nie is o-ver the o-cean,— my Bon-nie is o-ver the sea,— my Bon-nie is o-ver the o-cean,— oh bring back my Bon-nie to me! — Bring back, bring back, oh bring back my Bon-nie to me, to me, bring back, bring back, oh bring back my Bon-nie to me! —

Unit 2 Step 4

forty-five 45

Unit 3

⟨Photo page:
British school children⟩

▲ Children at a comprehensive school

At this boy's school the school colours are red and white.

Unit 3 Step 1

1 School uniform

blue black white grey
red yellow green brown

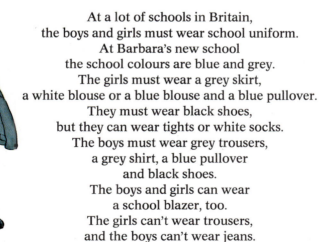

At a lot of schools in Britain,
the boys and girls must wear school uniform.
At Barbara's new school
the school colours are blue and grey.
The girls must wear a grey skirt,
a white blouse or a blue blouse and a blue pullover.
They must wear black shoes,
but they can wear tights or white socks.
The boys must wear grey trousers,
a grey shirt, a blue pullover
and black shoes.
The boys and girls can wear
a school blazer, too.
The girls can't wear trousers,
and the boys can't wear jeans.

1 Comprehension   *Answer the questions.*

1. What must the boys and girls wear at a lot of schools in Britain?
2. What are the school colours at Barbara's new school?
3. What must the girls wear?
4. What must the boys wear?
5. Can Barbara wear trousers at school?
6. Can the boys wear jeans?

forty-seven 47

Unit 3 Step 1

2 Colours

a) *Example:* What colour is the girl's skirt? – It's red.
   What colour are her tights? – They're blue.

b) *Example:* What's the girl wearing? – She's wearing …

c) OVER TO YOU What are you wearing? What's your neighbour wearing?

3 Ask your friends

Ronny and Kevin are at Barbara's school, too.
Make questions about their school uniform, and ask your friends.

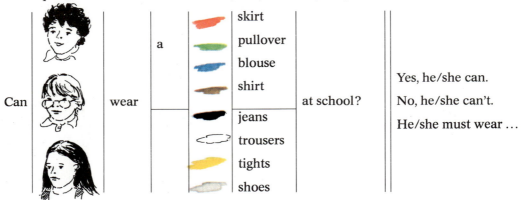

4 Can, can't or must   *Find the missing words.*

1. That window is dirty. I … clean it.
2. There's a chair. You … sit down.
3. It's raining. I … run.
4. There's Mrs Klein. I … say hello.
5. I … carry two buckets, but I … carry three.
   You … carry one for me.
6. I can't find my pencil.
   – You … have my pencil.
7. Can the girls wear trousers?
   – No, the girls … wear skirts.
8. What about the jeans over there?
   – No, you … wear jeans.
   You … wear trousers.
9. I'm German. – … you speak English?
10. Has Timmy got a lot of books?
    – Yes, but he … read.

Unit 3 Step 2

2 Homework

a) Barbara, Kevin and Ronny are all in 1B at Fulford Comprehensive School. They are in Ronny's bedroom. They are doing their homework together.

b) *Barbara:* I can't find my English textbook. Have you got it, Kevin?
Kevin: No, I haven't. But there's an English book on the floor.
Barbara: Oh, that's it. Thanks.

c) Kevin is doing an exercise. It is an English exercise.

Kevin: Oh dear. My exercise book is full. And I haven't got a new exercise book.
Ronny: You can have the old exercise book over there, Kevin. That isn't full.
Kevin: Oh, good. Thanks.

d) Ronny is doing an exercise, too. It is a German exercise.

Ronny: This question is difficult. I can't find the answer.
Barbara: That's an easy question.
Ronny: Easy for you, but not for me. You can speak German.
Barbara: Look at the example.
Ronny: Example? I can't see an example.
Barbara: Not on page twelve, on page eleven. You're doing the wrong exercise!

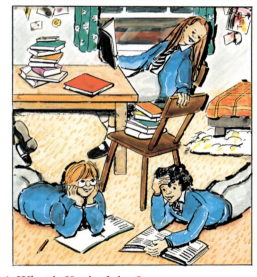

1 Comprehension

Answer the questions.

a) 1. What is Barbara's, Ronny's and Kevin's school?
2. Where are the friends today?
3. What are they doing?

b) 1. What can't Barbara find?
2. Has Kevin got it?
3. Where is it?

c) 1. What is Kevin doing?
2. Why can't he do his homework?
3. What can he have from Ronny?

d) 1. What is Ronny doing?
2. Why is the exercise easy for Barbara?
3. Why can't Ronny find the example?

forty-nine 49

Unit 3 Step 2

2 What's right?

a) *What is right* – **a** or **an**?   *Example:* **an** answer, **a** wrong answer; **a** box, **an** empty box.

… exercise book	… new exercise book	… question	… easy question
… page	… empty page	… example	… good example
… exercise	… difficult exercise	… German school	… English school
… answer	… right answer	… van	… old van
… book	… English book	… idea	… good idea

b) *Say the words with* **the** *([ðə] or [ði:]).*   *Example:* [ðə] *box,* [ði:] *empty box.*

3 Questions and answers

1. What's Kate carrying? –
   She's carrying an empty bucket.
2. And what about Kevin?
3. What's that on the floor?
4. And what's that on the chair?
5. What has Barbara got
   in her hand?
6. And what has her mother got?
7. What's Ronny wearing?
8. And what about Timmy?

4 Can you help?

a) *Find the right answers.*

1. Have you got my textbook?
2. I haven't got a biro.
3. Where's the example?
4. My exercise book is full.
5. Can you do this exercise?
6. What have we got for homework?
7. I can't find my school-bag.
8. Are we on page eight?

a) You can have my biro.
b) No, I can't. Let's ask the teacher.
c) There's a school-bag behind the door.
d) Yes, I have.
e) It's on page twenty.
f) No, we aren't. We're on page nine.
g) You can have my old exercise book.
h) Exercise two on page three.

b) *Can you find more answers? Work with your friend.*

3 Behind the door

a) It is Saturday afternoon, and it is raining.

Barbara: Let's go to my house.
We can play in my room.

b) Now the friends are at the Kleins' house.
Barbara's bedroom and the bathroom are on the right.
Her parents' bedroom and her sister's bedroom are on the left.

Kevin: What's that door with the window?
Barbara: We can't open it.
It hasn't got a handle.
But it's only an old cupboard.

c) *Ronny:* Hey, that's exciting!
Barbara: Oh, Ronny!
It's an empty cupboard.
Ronny: Let's look in.

Ronny can see stairs.
It is not a cupboard door.
It is the door to the attic.

d) Ronny can open the window but he cannot climb through.
He is too big.

Kevin: You can climb through, Kate.
You're small.
Kate: O.K. Put a table here.
Then I can stand on it.

Unit 3 Step 3

e) Kate is in the attic.
It is dark,
and it is dirty.
She can see a big box.

Kate:	There's a big box here.
Kevin:	What's in it?
Kate:	No idea. I can't open it.
Ronny:	Treasure!
Barbara:	Oh, Ronny!
Kate:	I'm coming down now.

f) But how can Kate get out?
The window is too high.
She cannot climb through.

Kate:	I can't get out!
Kevin:	What can we do?
Ronny:	Let's all push. Kate, can you pull?
Kate:	Yes, there's a handle here.
Ronny:	One, two, three, push!

g) But they cannot open the door.
Now Kate is kicking the door
because she is angry.

h) Bang – the door is open,
and Kate is on the floor.

Mrs Klein:	What are you doing?
Barbara:	Mum, it isn't a cupboard, it's the door to the attic.
Kate:	And there's a big box in the attic.
Kevin:	Can we play up there?
Ronny:	And look for the treasure in the box.
Mrs Klein:	Well, first clean the attic, and then you can open the big box.

Unit 3 Step 3

1 Comprehension: Right or wrong?

Make the wrong sentences right.
Examples: 1. It is Saturday afternoon.   "That's right."
              The sun is shining.   "That's wrong. It's raining."

2. The friends are in Kevin's flat.
   The door with the window hasn't got a handle.
3. Ronny can see a room.
   The door is a cupboard door.
4. Ronny can't climb through because he is too small.
   Kate must stand on a chair.
5. Kate can see a small box.
   She can open the box.
6. Kate can't climb through the window.
   Kate is pulling the door.
7. Ronny is kicking the door.
   Kate is angry.
8. First they can open the box – then they must clean the attic.

2 What are they doing?

a) Who can you see in the pictures?
b) Where is he/she? Where are they?
c) What's he/she doing? What are they doing?

Example: 1. a) I can see Kevin.
          b) He's in bed.
          c) He's reading.

3 Yes and no
Answer the questions.   *Examples:* **Is** Kate Kevin's sister? – Yes, she **is**.
                    Have the Bennetts got a shop? – No, they **haven't**.
                      Can Timmy read? – No, he **can't**.

1. Can Barbara wear trousers at school?
2. Has Ronny got a brother?
3. Is his brother's name Tommy?
4. Have the Bennetts got two taxis?
5. Has the Kleins' house got an attic?
6. Are Kevin and Ronny good friends?
7. Can Barbara speak German?
8. Are the Bennetts from Leeds?
9. Has Barbara got a brother?
10. Is Kate big?
11. Is Barbara's father in Germany?
12. Can Mrs Bennett drive a taxi?

fifty-three 53

Unit 3 Step 3

4 Because

a) 1. The friends can't play in the road
   2. They can't open the door
   3. Ronny can't climb through the window
   4. But Kate can climb through
   5. Kate can see the big box
   6. Kate can't get out
   7. Kate is kicking the door

BECAUSE

... the window is too high.
... she's small.
... it's raining.   ... it hasn't got a handle.
... she's in the attic now.
... she's angry.   ... he's too big.

b) 1. Why can't Barbara wear jeans at school?
   2. Why is German homework easy for Barbara?
   3. Why can she speak German?
   4. Why can't Barbara find her textbook?
   5. Why can't Ronny see the example?
   6. Why can't Timmy watch TV in the evening?

BECAUSE

... she can speak German.
... girls must wear skirts.
... it's under her chair.
... he's only two.
... her father is German.
... he's looking at the wrong page.

5 The dirty attic

Look at the pictures and say what the friends are doing.

Picture 1: What is there in the attic?   There is ... There are ...
          What must the friends do?   They must clean/put ...
Picture 2: What have the friends got?   Ronny has got a ... Kate ...
          What are the friends doing?   ... is sitting/standing/cleaning/putting ...
Picture 3: What about the attic now?   The ... is clean.
          What are the friends doing?   ... is carrying/pulling/pushing ...
          What is dirty now?   Kevin's trousers are ..., Ronny's ... is ...

6 Behind Ronny's house

Say what they are doing.

Examples: make – new house for Timmy Ronny is making a new house for Timmy.
clean – old chair He is cleaning an old chair.
carry – empty bucket He is carrying an empty bucket.

1. sit in – empty box
   read – English magazine
   wear – red blouse

2. write – new exercise book
   do – easy exercise
   wear – yellow skirt

3. sit on – old bucket
   read – German comic
   wear – old pullover

4. sit at – red table; play with – toy car; wear – old shirt

7 Opposites Find the opposites. Example: left – right.

easy	– ?	Mr	– ?	full	– ?	father	– ?
in front of	– ?	sister	– ?	old	– ?	black	– ?
on	– ?	clean	– ?	big	– ?	man	– ?
girl	– ?	question	– ?	wrong	– ?	the sun is shining	– ?

8 Look, listen and say

sit	the Kleins' car		trousers
speak	Ronny's pullover	[z]	magazine
must	the girls' cardigans		easy
test			is
sister	[s] Kate's brother		has
	Mr Bennett's taxi		please
	her parents' shop		

[s] - [z]
This exercise is easy.
Tom's trousers are too small.
Ronny hasn't got a sister.
This isn't our register.
Susan's school blazer is blue.
The girls' skirts are red.

[ʌ] - [æ]
Come on, Andy.
Carry the bucket into the attic.
The sponge and the brush
are in the flat.

There's a black cat under the van.
That's lucky.
A taxi is standing in front of
the school.

Unit 3 Step 3

THE ALPHABET

⟨The alphabet song⟩

This is ALPHA.
He can spell English words.

Can you spell your name?

Spell some English words.

sister   taxi   idea
brother van   funny
sometimes friend evening

The secret

In a dark, dark road there's a dark, dark house.
In the dark, dark house there's a dark, dark room.
In the dark, dark room there's a dark, dark cupboard.
In the dark, dark cupboard there's a dark, dark box.
And in the dark, dark box there's a … secret.

⟨**Authentic Britain: Signs**⟩

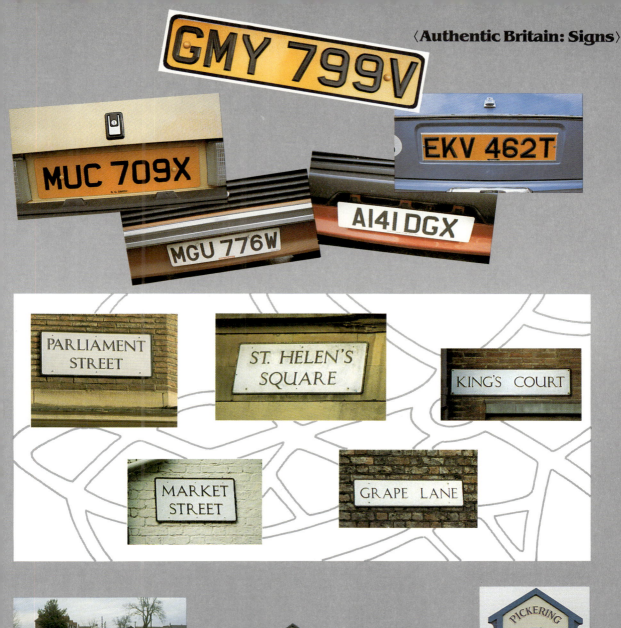

Unit 4 Step 1

TANGRAM Unit 4 PUZZLES

1

1. This is a TANGRAM puzzle. TANGRAM puzzles have got seven pieces. Ronny is making pictures for Timmy. He can make a lot of pictures with the pieces.

2. Look, Timmy, this is a house and that's a bridge.

3. This is a cat.
   It's looking at you, Timmy.

   That's a horse.
   It's looking at the cat.

4. These are two bridges…

   and those are two houses.

5. These are two horses.
   They're standing together.

   Those are two cats.
   They're looking at us.

6. *Ronny:* What are these ducks doing, Timmy?
   Timmy: They are swimming.
   Ronny: And those ducks?
   Timmy: Those aren't ducks. Those are hens.

7. These children are playing hopscotch.

   Those children are reading comics.

8. These men are riding on horses.

   Those men are playing football.

9. These women are dancing.

   Those women are dancing, too.

58 *fifty-eight*

1 Timmy's picture-book

Timmy is looking at his picture-book with Ronny.

a) "This is a car and that's a van."

b) "These are cats and those are…"

⟨c)⟩ "This man is going for a walk."
(that … these … those)

going for a walk / swimming / playing hopscotch / playing football / reading a book / riding a horse

2 Look, listen and say

a) a duck	seven duck**s**	[S]	a hen	six hen**s**	[Z]
a map	ten map**s**		a pencil	nine pencil**s**	
a shirt	four shirt**s**		a pullover	three pullover**s**	
b) a horse	eight horse**s**	[IZ]	one brush – two brush**es**		a house [haʊs] –
a page	five page**s**				⚠ two houses ['haʊzɪz]
a blouse	two blouse**s**		one box – two box**es**		

c) *Look at these words and say them:*

one child	– two **children**	one lady	– two lad**ies**
one man	– two **men**	one baby	– two bab**ies**
one woman	– two **women**	one family	– two famil**ies**

d) *Can you say these?*

cats and dogs
socks and shoes
    flats and houses
    roads and bridges

2 Over and out

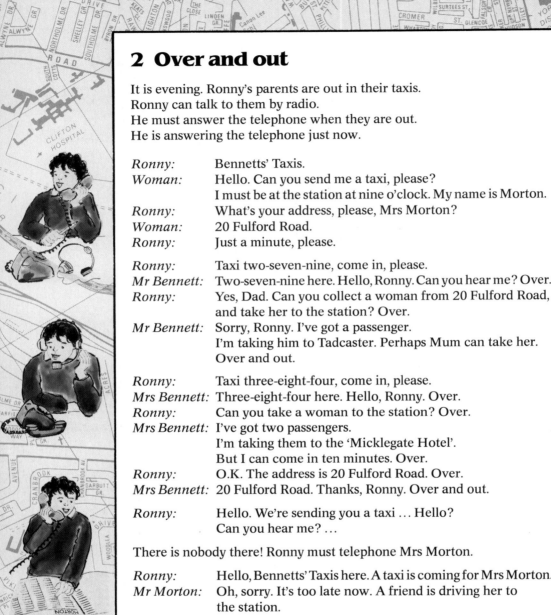

It is evening. Ronny's parents are out in their taxis.
Ronny can talk to them by radio.
He must answer the telephone when they are out.
He is answering the telephone just now.

Ronny:	Bennetts' Taxis.	5
Woman:	Hello. Can you send me a taxi, please?	
	I must be at the station at nine o'clock. My name is Morton.	
Ronny:	What's your address, please, Mrs Morton?	
Woman:	20 Fulford Road.	
Ronny:	Just a minute, please.	10
Ronny:	Taxi two-seven-nine, come in, please.	
Mr Bennett:	Two-seven-nine here. Hello, Ronny. Can you hear me? Over.	
Ronny:	Yes, Dad. Can you collect a woman from 20 Fulford Road, and take her to the station? Over.	
Mr Bennett:	Sorry, Ronny. I've got a passenger.	15
	I'm taking him to Tadcaster. Perhaps Mum can take her. Over and out.	
Ronny:	Taxi three-eight-four, come in, please.	
Mrs Bennett:	Three-eight-four here. Hello, Ronny. Over.	
Ronny:	Can you take a woman to the station? Over.	20
Mrs Bennett:	I've got two passengers.	
	I'm taking them to the 'Micklegate Hotel'.	
	But I can come in ten minutes. Over.	
Ronny:	O.K. The address is 20 Fulford Road. Over.	
Mrs Bennett:	20 Fulford Road. Thanks, Ronny. Over and out.	25
Ronny:	Hello. We're sending you a taxi … Hello? Can you hear me? …	

There is nobody there! Ronny must telephone Mrs Morton.

Ronny:	Hello, Bennetts' Taxis here. A taxi is coming for Mrs Morton.	
Mr Morton:	Oh, sorry. It's too late now. A friend is driving her to the station.	30

1 Comprehension   *Right or wrong?*

Examples: It is evening.   – "That's right."
            Ronny's parents are at home. – "That's wrong. They're out in their taxis."

1. Ronny can talk to his parents by radio.
2. Mrs Morton must be in Tadcaster at nine o'clock.
3. Mrs Morton's address is 20 Fulford Road.
4. Mr Bennett can collect her.
5. Mr Bennett is driving to Tadcaster.
6. Mrs Bennett is taking a passenger to the station.
7. She cannot collect Mrs Morton.
8. Mrs Morton is still waiting for the taxi.

Unit 4 Step 2

2 Who is saying what?

3 Can you do it?

Put in *me, you, him, her, it, us* or *them*.

Example: This *exercise* isn't difficult. Can you do *it*?

1. *Kate and Kevin* are coming. I can hear … .
2. *I* must go to the station. Can you send … a taxi?
3. *This box* is too big. I can't carry … .
4. *We*'re late. Can you drive … to school, Dad?
5. Dad, *Kevin* can't do his homework. Can you help …?
6. Are *you* going for a walk? Can I come with …?
7. *Kate* is coming. Let's wait for … .
8. Where are *you,* Kate and Kevin? We can't see … .

4 Role Play Can you take me to . . . ?

Passenger to Mr Bennett: Can you take me to Tadcaster, please?
Mr Bennett to passenger: Tadcaster? Yes, I can take you there.
Mr Bennett to Ronny: Ronny, can you hear me? I've got a passenger. I'm taking him to Tadcaster. Over.
Ronny: Tadcaster? O.K. I've got it. Over and out.

62 sixty-two

3 The box in the attic

a) The four friends are at Barbara's house
Barbara's mother is going out.

Barbara: Can we open the box
in the attic today, Mum?
Mrs Klein: Is the attic clean now?
Barbara: Yes, it is.
Mrs Klein: O.K. then. I'm going out now.
Goodbye.

b) The box is old,
and it is not easy to open.
The children must push and pull.
Now the box is open.
But there is no treasure in the box.
Only old clothes.
And old clothes are not very exciting.

Kate: Never mind. Let's take them out.
Perhaps we can play with them.

c) Kate has got a black jacket on,
and black trousers.
Barbara has got an old uniform on.
Kevin is wearing a long dress.
And Ronny has got a coat on, and
a big black hat.
Not bad!

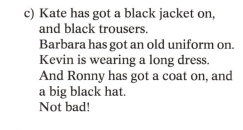

d) But downstairs there are two people
at the door, a man and a girl...

sixty-three 63

Unit 4 Step 3

e) Ronny: Ssh! What's that?
   Kate: I can hear someone downstairs.
   Barbara: It can't be my mother. She's out.
   Kevin: Let's telephone the police.
   Barbara: We can't. The telephone is downstairs.

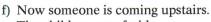

f) Now someone is coming upstairs.
   The children are afraid.
   What can they do? Kate has got an idea.
   Kate: Listen, Ronny!
         When he's in front of the door, you must throw your coat over his head. Then he can't see us.
         Kevin, you must push him onto the floor.
   Kevin: Then you and Barbara can sit on him.
   Kate.: Ssh. He's in front of the door.
          One – two – three – now!

g) Now the coat is on the floor.
   The man is sitting up. He is very angry.
   Man: Verdammt nochmal!
        Was fällt euch denn ein?
   Barbara: Dad!
   Girl: Was ist los da oben?
   Barbara: Elke!
   Ronny: Oh no! It's Barbara's father and her sister from Germany.

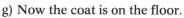

Unit 4 Step 3

1 Comprehension *Answer the questions.*

a) Where are the friends?
   What can they do today?

b) Why must they push and pull?
   What is there in the box?

c) What have the friends got on?

d) Who is at the door?

e) What can Kate hear?
   Why can't it be Mrs Klein?
   Why can't they telephone the police?

f) Why are the children afraid?
   Kate has an idea – what must Ronny do?
   And what must Kevin do?

g) What is the man doing now?
   Who is the man? Who is the girl?

2 Find the right word
(me, you, him, her, it, us, them)

a) 1. Kevin, where are you? I can't see … .
   2. Where's the box? – Dad has got … .
   3. We're late. Can you send … a taxi?
   4. Where's Timmy? I can't find … .
   5. Hello, Ronny. Can you hear … ?
   6. Kevin and Kate are cleaning the van.
      Let's help … .
   7. A woman is waiting at the hotel.
      Can you send … a taxi?
   8. I can drive … to the station,
      Mr and Mrs Pearson.

b) 1. There's Mr Pearson. Let's wait for … .
   2. Ronny, read … a comic, please.
   3. Look, the Kleins. – Where? I can't see … .
   4. My mother can collect … in five minutes,
      Mrs Morton.
   5. There's Elke. Let's talk to … .
   6. We're going to York. – Can you take …
      to the station?
   7. Barbara and Ronny, I can give … back
      your exercise books.
   8. The van is dirty. I must clean … .

3 Elke

What is Elke doing?
Example: In picture number one she is looking at a map.

to do, to answer, to go, to look at, to play, to talk to, to read, to listen to

sixty-five 65

Unit 4 Step 3

4 People in front of the shop

a) *Who is there in front of the shop?*
1. In front of the shop there's a woman.
2. Then there's a woman with a baby.
3. ...

⟨b⟩ *What are they doing?*
1. The woman is carrying a box.
2. The woman is going for a ... with ... .
3. ...

⟨c⟩ *What are they wearing?*
1. The woman is wearing ... .
2. ...

⟨5 What is the right word?⟩

in front of   from   in   onto
on (2x)   upstairs   out   downstairs   over   at (2x)

Find the right words.

1. The children are ... Barbara's house.
2. Barbara's mother is going ... .
3. There are old clothes ... the box.
4. Kevin is funny – he has got a dress ... .
5. Two people are ... the door.
6. Kate can hear someone ... .
7. The children are afraid because someone is coming ... .
8. When the man is ... the door, Ronny must throw the coat ... his head.
9. Kevin must push him ... the floor.
10. The girls can sit ... him.
11. But the man is angry – he is Barbara's father ... Germany.

⟨6 What can I wear, Mum?⟩

What can I wear, Mum?
These tights are dirty.
  Those tights are too small!
This skirt is new.
  That ...

Unit 4 Step 3

7 What has Timmy got?

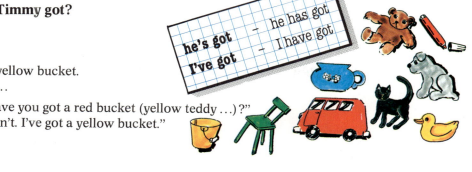

a) He's got a yellow bucket.
He's got a …

b) "Timmy, have you got a red bucket (yellow teddy …)?"
"No, I haven't. I've got a yellow bucket."

8 Hello

Ask your friends.

⟨9 Elke and Barbara⟩

a) Barbara is telling her sister about her new friends.
"I've got three new friends. Their names are … .
Ronny's house is … . His father … ."

Now you go on.

b) *Now talk about your friends.*

⟨10 Let's sing a song: He's got the whole world in His hand⟩

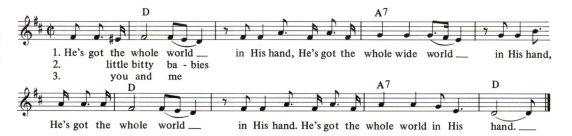

1. He's got the whole world — in His hand, He's got the whole wide world — in His hand,
2. little bitty ba-bies
3. you and me

He's got the whole world — in His hand. He's got the whole world in His hand. —

Unit 5

⟨Photo page:
At the breakfast table⟩

English families often have cornflakes, toast and marmalade, and bacon, eggs and sausages for breakfast.

Unit 5 Step 1

1 Numbers

0 oh	1 one	2 two	3 three	4 four	5 five	6 six	7 seven	8 eight	9 nine
10 ten	11 eleven	12 twelve	13 thirteen	14 fourteen	15 fifteen	16 sixteen	17 seventeen	18 eighteen	19 nineteen
20 twenty	21 twenty-one	22 twenty-two	23 twenty-three	24 twenty-four	25 twenty-five	26 twenty-six	27 twenty-seven	28 twenty-eight	29 twenty-nine
30 thirty	31 thirty-one	32 thirty-two	33 thirty-three	34	35	36	37	38	39
40 forty	41	42	43	44 forty-four	45	46	47	48	49
50 fifty	51	52	53	54	55 fifty-five	56	57	58	59
60 sixty	61	62	63	64	65	66 sixty-six	67	68	69
70 seventy	71	72	73	74	75	76	77 seventy-seven	78	79
80 eighty	81	82	83	84	85	86	87	88 eighty-eight	89
90 ninety	91	92	93	94	95	96	97	98	99 ninety-nine
100 a/one hundred	101 a hundred and one								
200 two hundred									

1 What are they saying?

"How old is your sister?" "She's 16."

"Can you take me to 81, Selby Road?"

"How old is your dad?" "He's 35." "My dad is 43."

"Open your books at page 92, please."

"How can I get to Leeds Road?" "Take a number 42 bus."

"Look at the exercise on page 78, please."

"There are 25 pictures in Timmy's new book."

"29 Denmark Road, please."

"Where can I get the number 64 bus, please?" "Over there."

sixty-nine 69

Unit 5 Step 2

2 The bus driver

A reporter from a newspaper in York is talking to Wendy Webb about her job.

a) *Reporter:* You're a bus driver, Mrs Webb?
   Wendy: Yes, I drive a school bus.
   Reporter: You collect the children from the villages?
   Wendy: Yes, I collect them every morning,
      and I take them to school.
      To Fulford Comprehensive School in York.
   Reporter: You get up early then?
   Wendy: Yes, because I start at half past seven.
      We get to school at quarter to nine.
   Reporter: And in the afternoon?
   Wendy: Well, I drive to Fulford again at quarter to four,
      and I wait for the children.
      They come out at four o'clock.
      Then I take them home.
   Reporter: And then you go home?
   Wendy: Well, no. At quarter past five I clean the bus.
      I often find a lot of things in the bus.

1 Wendy Webb

You are Wendy Webb.

1. I get up …
2. I start …
3. I collect …
4. I take …
5. We get to school …
6. I drive to Fulford again …
7. I wait for …
8. They come out …
9. I take …
10. I clean …

a) the children from the villages.
b) early.
c) the children to school.
d) at half past seven.
e) the children.
f) at quarter to nine.
g) at quarter to four.
h) the children home.
i) the bus.
j) at four o'clock.

Then I go home!

70   *seventy*

Unit 5 Step 2

b) The next day Wendy reads in the newspaper:

BUS DRIVER WANTS TO HOLD JUMBLE SALE

Wendy Webb is a bus driver. She collects the children from the villages and takes them to Fulford Comprehensive School in York. She starts at half past seven every morning and they get to school at quarter to nine. In the afternoon she drives to Fulford again at 4 o'clock and takes the children home. At quarter past five she cleans the bus. She often finds a lot of things in the bus.

"The children sometimes collect their things the next day," says Wendy. "But I've still got a lot of things." She has got pencils, felt pens, comics, exercise books, rulers, coats, pullovers, right shoes and left shoes.

"Now I want to hold a jumble sale!" says Wendy.

2 Wendy's job

1. **I get up** early.
2. I **start** at half past seven every morning.
3. I **collect** the children from the villages.
4. I **take** them to Fulford Comprehensive School.
5. I always **get** there at quarter to nine.
6. In the afternoon I **drive** to Fulford again.
7. Then I **take** the children home.
8. At quarter past five I **clean** the bus.
9. I often **find** things in the bus.
10. I …

She gets up early.
She … at half past seven every morning.
She … the children from the villages.
She … them to school.
She always … there at quarter to nine.
In the afternoon she … to Fulford again.
She … .
Then she … the bus.
She often … things in the bus.
She **wants** to hold a jumble sale.

"Half past six?
What about **Kevin**?"
"And **Kate**?"
They mustn't be late for **school**.
"And on Sundays?"
"The children, too?" "Well, sometimes

"I   get up at half past six."
You get up very early, Mr Pearson.
"**He gets** up at eight o'clock."
"**She gets** up at eight o'clock, too."
It   **starts** at nine o'clock."
"We get up at nine o'clock on Sundays."
they get up at ten o'clock on Sundays."

seventy-one 71

Unit 5 Step 2

3 What time is it, please?

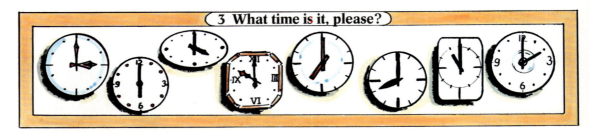

4 "Past" and "to"

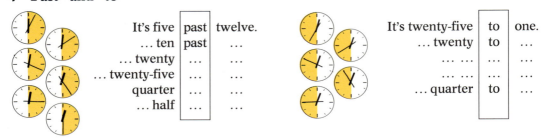

It's five	past	twelve.		It's twenty-five	to	one.
… ten	past	…		… twenty	to	…
… twenty	…	…		… …	…	…
… twenty-five	…	…		… …	…	…
… quarter	…	…		… quarter	to	…
… half	…	…				

Say what time it is.
a) 4.10   1.25   6.15   b) 5.50   8.55   2.45   c) 4.15   2.40   9.25
   5.20   3.05   2.30   10.45   3.40   9.35   7.45   5.10   3.30

d) *You can also say "four-ten."* `4:10`

5 Wendy's jumble sale

Example: "How many biros has Wendy got?"
"She's got sixteen."

3 Kate's kite

Kate has got a new kite.
She goes to the park with Barbara.
There is a man in the park with his dog.
He wants to teach it a new trick.
The girls watch.

First the man throws his stick.
The dog runs after the stick, picks it up
and carries it back to the man.
The man gives the dog a biscuit.
He says "Good boy" and does it again.

Then Kate and Barbara start to play with
the kite.
Kate holds the string
and Barbara holds the kite.

Then Kate runs
and the kite flies into the air.
But it falls down again.

The dog sees it, picks it up
and runs away with it.
The girls run after the dog.
It carries the kite to the man
because it wants a biscuit.

Kate and Barbara are very angry.
The kite has got a big hole in it.
The man is very sorry.
He says, "Never mind.
I can make you a new kite."

Unit 5 Step 3

1 Comprehension

What is right here? Put the sentences together.

1. The man throws the stick.
2. The dog carries the stick back to the man.
3. The girls watch the man and his dog.
4. Barbara holds the kite.
5. The kite flies into the air.
6. The dog sees the kite.
7. The dog runs away with the kite.
8. The girls are angry.

a) Then they play with the kite.
b) Then it picks it up.
c) Then the dog runs after it.
d) Then the man says he can make them a new kite.
e) Then the man gives the dog a biscuit.
f) Then the girls run after the dog.
g) Then Kate runs with it.
h) Then it falls down.

2 Look, listen and say

to throw to find to drive	she throw**s** he find**s** Wendy drive**s**	[z]
to pick to get	he/she/it pick**s** the dog get**s**	[s]
to watch to teach to push	he watch**es** he teach**es** she push**es**	[ɪz]

3 What you hear, what you write

to **fl**y	it **fl**ies	[flaɪz]
to ca**rr**y	he ca**rr**ies	[ˈkærɪz]
to p**l**ay	she p**l**ays	[pleɪz]
to **s**ay	she **s**ays	[sez]
to **g**o	it **g**oes	[gəʊz]
to **d**o	he **d**oes	[dʌz]

4 Ken, Bob and the ball

Ken often ... his dog Bob new tricks.
First Ken ... his ball.

Then Bob ... after the ball
and ... it up.

Then he ... the ball back to Ken.
Ken ... "Good dog."

Then Ken ... the ball again.
But there is a house, and a window is open.
Bob ... the ball, but he cannot run after it –

– because the ball ... through the open window.
So Ken ... to the house.
But there is nobody there. So he must wait.

> to teach
> to throw

> to run
> to pick

> to carry
> to say

> to throw
> to watch

> to fly
> to go

4 Bonzo the dog

Hello, children.
I'm Bonzo. My people are the Wilsons – Mrs Wilson
and Mr Wilson and their children Peter and Mandy.

Peter is my pet. Every morning I wake him up
at quarter past seven and wash his face. 5
Then he washes his face again and makes my breakfast.
After that, Peter has breakfast, too.

When Peter is at school, I often take his mother
for a walk in the park. She always gets lost there.
Then she shouts my name. But I always find her. 10

At twelve o'clock Mrs Wilson gives me my lunch.
Fred, the cat sometimes comes over the wall,
but I always bark at him and then he runs away.

On Saturdays Peter and I play with our friends.
I teach the boys a lot of tricks. 15
For example, when I bring a stick, they throw it for me.
When I run after them, they ride away
on their bikes.

Unit 5 Step 4

Every Sunday we go out in the car.
I sometimes see dogs in the other cars. 20
Then I bark at them, and they bark at me, too.
That's great!

After tea my people often watch TV.
Then we play a game.
I sit in front of the TV and they throw shoes at me. 25
I pick them up and take them into Peter's bedroom.
I like shoes.

At nine o'clock I take Peter to bed. He's a good boy,
so he can always sleep in my bed.

1 Comprehension *Can you go on?*

1. Bonzo wakes Peter up at …
2. Peter makes Bonzo's …
3. Bonzo always takes Mrs Wilson …
4. Mrs Wilson always gets lost …
5. At 12 o'clock Mrs Wilson gives Bonzo …
6. When Bonzo barks at the cat, he …
7. On Saturdays Peter and Bonzo play …
8. Bonzo teaches the boys …
9. Every Sunday the Wilsons go out …
10. Bonzo watches …
11. When Bonzo sits in front of the TV, the Wilsons throw …
12. Bonzo takes the shoes into …
13. Bonzo and Peter go to bed at …
14. Peter can sleep in …

2 Bonzo and Peter *Put in the missing words.*

a) 1. *(wake)* Bonzo **wakes** Peter up.
   2. *(wash)* Peter … his face.
   3. *(go)* Peter and Bonzo … downstairs.
   4. *(make)* Peter … Bonzo's breakfast.
b) 1. *(go)* Bonzo and Mrs Wilson … for a walk.
   2. *(get)* Bonzo always … lost.
   3. *(shout)* Mrs Wilson … his name.
   4. *(go)* They … home for lunch.
c) 1. *(bring)* Bonzo … a stick.
   2. *(throw)* The boys … it for him.
   3. *(ride)* They … their bikes.
   4. *(run)* Bonzo … after them.
d) 1. *(do)* After tea Peter … his homework.
   2. *(watch)* Then the Wilsons … TV.
   3. *(watch)* Bonzo … TV, too.
   4. *(go)* Then Peter and Bonzo … to bed.

Unit 5 Step 4

3 On Mondays

Say when you do it.
On Mondays –

I wake up at ...
I get up at ...
I have breakfast at ...

I go to school at ...
School starts at ...
I come out of school at ...

I have lunch at ...
I do my homework at ...
I have tea at ...
I go to bed at ...

4 On Sundays

a) *What about Sundays?*
Say what you do on Sundays. On Sundays I

go for a 🏞 watch 📺 ride my 🚲 go to ⛪
play 🃏 go out in the 🚗 play ⚽
read 📖 listen to the 📻 play with my 🐕🐈
have breakfast in 🛏

b) *What about your friend?* He/she ...

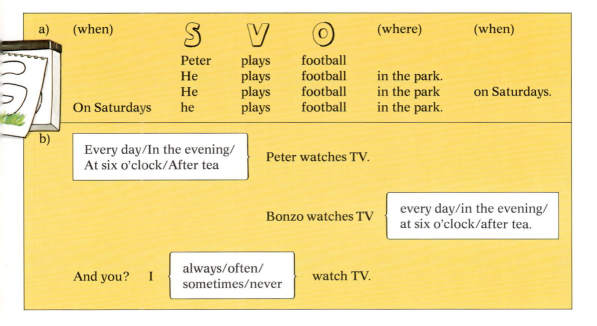

a)	(when)	S	V	O	(where)	(when)
		Peter	plays	football		
		He	plays	football	in the park.	
		He	plays	football	in the park	on Saturdays.
	On Saturdays	he	plays	football	in the park.	

b) Every day/In the evening/At six o'clock/After tea — Peter watches TV.

Bonzo watches TV — every day/in the evening/at six o'clock/after tea.

And you? I — always/often/sometimes/never — watch TV.

seventy-seven 77

Unit 5 Step 4

5 The days of the week

6 Look, listen and say

[s] – [z]

Ronny collects his parents' books.
Barbara's mother sometimes reads German newspapers.
Ronny takes the bags and puts them
in the Bennetts' taxi.
Kate has got the boys' magazines.
You can get biros and pencils in the Pearsons' shop, too.

⟨**7 Let's sing a song: I am a music man**⟩

Unit 5 Step 4

8

Look at the pictures and find the right sentences.
Example: The right sentence for picture 1 is:
A good dog comes when you shout its name.

a) Dogs often watch TV with the family.
b) Sometimes dogs can teach you new tricks.
c) It is not easy to get the right dog.
d) A good dog comes when you shout its name.
e) Sometimes dogs are ill.
f) Some dogs can read.
g) A dog always wants to play.
h) Dogs often bark at you.
i) A good dog wakes you up when there is someone in the house.

seventy-nine 79

Unit 6

⟨Photo page: Whitby⟩

Whitby Harbour

Whitby Harbour

Whitby Sands

Whitby Bay

Unit 6 Step 1

1 By train to Whitby

a) The four friends are going home from school.
   The next day is Saturday.
   They are talking about their plans.
   "What about a picnic?" says Barbara.
   "No, let's go to the seaside," says Kate. 5
   "Why can't we go to the Railway Museum?" says Kevin.
   "Well, I want to make a kite and fly it," says Ronny.

b) The children go into Ronny's house.
   Ronny's dad is playing with Timmy.
   They tell Mr Bennett about their different plans. 10
"What can we do?" asks Barbara. "Where can we go?"
"What about Whitby?" answers Mr Bennett.
"I can't take you there. But perhaps Elke can go
with you. You can go by bus to Pickering,
15 then by train to Whitby. It's a very old train."
"The seaside! Great!" says Kate.
"Good idea!" says Kevin. "I like old trains!"
"And we can have a picnic on the beach," shouts Barbara.
"And I can fly my kite," shouts Ronny.
20 "Good," says Mr Bennett. "Now everybody is happy."

c) But not everybody is happy. Timmy is crying.
   "What's the matter, Timmy?" asks Ronny.
   "I want to go, too," cries Timmy.
   "We can look after him, Dad," says Ronny.
25 "O.K. then. Timmy can go, too."

1 Comprehension

1. The four friends have different plans.
   Barbara wants to have …;
   Kate wants to …;
   Kevin …;
   Ronny … .
2. How can the children go from York to Pickering?
3. And from Pickering to Whitby?

4. Kevin thinks Whitby is a good idea because…;
   Barbara thinks Whitby is a good idea because…;
   Ronny …;
   Kate … .
5. Who can look after the children?
6. And who can look after Timmy?
7. Are they all happy now?

Unit 6 Step 1

2 Time for bed

Ronny and Timmy are playing together.
At half past seven Ronny says, "Come on, Timmy, time for bed now."
"Can't I watch TV?" …Timmy,
but Ronny …, "Sorry, Timmy. It's too late."
So Timmy … his cars and his ball into his box.
Next Ronny … Timmy's face and hands.
After that Timmy … into his bed,
and Ronny … him a story.
Then Ronny … "Good night,"
… downstairs and … his kite.

3 What are the others doing?

Now Ronny is making his kite.
But what are the others doing?

Well,

Barbara	is taking a passenger to the station.
Mr Bennett	is playing with his teddy.
Kevin and Kate	are dancing.
The Kleins	are cleaning the shop.
Mr and Mrs Pearson	are reading comics.
Timmy	is writing a letter to a friend in Germany.

Wait a minute, that's all wrong. What _are_ they doing?

4 Who?

Look at the pictures in exercise 3, then answer the questions.

Examples:
"Who is taking a passenger to the station?" "Mr Bennett is."
"Who is reading comics?" "Kevin and Kate are."

1. Who is writing a letter to a friend in Germany?
2. Who is cleaning the shop?
3. Who is dancing?
4. Who is playing with his teddy?
5. Who is making a kite?

2 Picnic food

a) It is Friday evening. The children are all at Barbara's house.
They are talking about their picnic.

Barbara: What have we got for our picnic, Elke?
Elke: We've got sandwiches, apples and a packet of biscuits.
5 *Kevin:* What have you got, Ronny?
Ronny: I've got sandwiches, an orange and a bar of chocolate.
Barbara: What about Kate and Kevin?
Kate: We've got sandwiches, bananas and a big bottle of lemonade.
Elke: Be careful with the bottle, Kate.
10 *Kate:* I'm always careful!

b) *Ronny:* I'm hungry!
Elke: Have a biscuit.
Ronny: Thanks.
Elke: What about you, Kevin?
15 *Kevin:* No, thanks. I'm not hungry.
But I'm thirsty. Can I have a glass of lemonade?
Elke: Sorry, it's all gone.

1 What goes together?

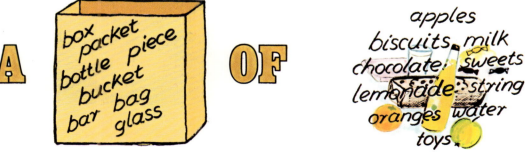

How many can you find?   *Example:* a bottle of lemonade
a bottle of water

Unit 6 Step 2

2 Role Play Have a...

a) Have
- a piece of chocolate.
- a sandwich.
- a glass of milk.
- ...

Thanks/Thank you.

No, thanks. I'm not hungry/thirsty.

b) Can I have
- a sweet
- an apple
- a banana
- ...
, please

Here you are.

Sorry, they're all gone.

3 Make a kite – it's easy!

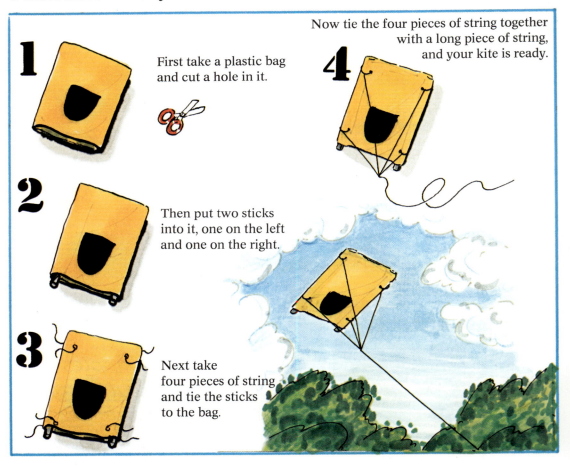

1 First take a plastic bag and cut a hole in it.

2 Then put two sticks into it, one on the left and one on the right.

3 Next take four pieces of string and tie the sticks to the bag.

4 Now tie the four pieces of string together with a long piece of string, and your kite is ready.

3 Seaside Special

a) Poor Timmy! He is ill. He cannot go to Whitby with the children. He is very unhappy.
"Never mind," says Ronny. "You can have my radio."

b) Mr Bennett drives the friends to the
5   bus station, and they take the bus
    to Pickering. At Pickering they get
    into the old train and sit down.
    The train starts. Kevin opens the
    window. A lot of smoke comes in,
10 and Kevin gets a dirty face.
    Poor Kevin! The others laugh at him.

c) At Whitby the sun is shining.
   They get out of the train
   and go down to the beach.
   "Who's first at the sea!" shouts Kate. 15
   She starts to run – and falls over a
   stone. The bag flies through the air
   and falls onto another stone.
   The bottle breaks. Poor Kate!
   "Oh dear," she says, "lemonade   20
   sandwiches for lunch!"

Unit 6   Step 3

d) Now Ronny and Kevin are playing with the kite. It is windy on the beach.
Ronny throws his kite into the air and Kevin pulls the string. It is a good kite.
It flies high into the air.
25 "Be careful," shouts Ronny. "It's very windy!"
Too late – the string breaks. And the kite falls into the sea.
Poor Ronny.

e) An hour later. The friends are swimming.
The sea is blue. But the water isn't very warm.
30 And when Barbara comes out, she is blue, too –
blue with cold. Poor Barbara.
The children put on their clothes and go back
to the road. Now it is raining.
They see a van with 'BBC' on it.
35 "What's happening?" says Barbara.
"No idea. Let's go and see," says Elke.

f) "Hello, everybody. This is 'Seaside Special'.
Today we're in Whitby, and it's raining again.
Let's have our first request.
40 A boy is standing here.
What's your name, please?"
"Ronny Bennett."
"Where are you from, Ronny?"
"I'm from York."
45 "And what's your request?"
"Can you play 'The sun has got his hat on'
for my brother Timmy? He's ill
and he's at home in bed."
"O.K. Timmy Bennett, are you listening?
50 The first request is for you …"

Well – somebody is happy.

Unit 6 Step 3

1 Comprehension

Answer the questions.
a) Why can't Timmy go to Whitby?
   Say what Ronny gives him.
b) Say how the friends get to Whitby.
   Say what Kevin does in the train.
   Say why Kate laughs.
c) Say why the bag flies through the air.
   What happens to the bottle?
d) What are Kevin and Ronny doing?
   Why must Kevin be careful?
   What happens to the kite?
e) It is an hour later. What are the friends doing now?
   Say what they see when they go back to the road.
f) Say what questions the man asks Ronny.
   What is Ronny's request?

2 Elke's photos

What is everybody doing in the photos?
Example: In picture number one the children are getting into Mr. Bennett's taxi.

3 Questions and answers

a) *Find the right answers to the questions.*
1. What have we got for lunch?
2. How many apples are there?
3. Are you hungry, too?
4. Where are the sandwiches?
5. Who has got the red bag?
6. Can you carry my bag a minute?
7. Is Ronny still swimming?
8. Why aren't you swimming?
9. When must we go home?

a) Yes, I am.
b) They're in the red bag.
c) Barbara has got it.
d) There are four.
e) We've got sandwiches and apples.
f) No, he isn't. He's putting on his clothes.
g) At five o'clock.
h) Yes, I can.
i) Because it's too cold.

b) *Can you give different answers to the questions?*

eighty-seven   87

Unit 6 Step 3

4 What Barbara does, what you do

Barbara gets up at ten to eight every morning.
She has breakfast.
Then she puts on her coat
and goes to school.

Sometimes she goes on her bike.
but sometimes she walks.
She gets to school at ten minutes to nine.
I get up at …

5 On the beach and at the station

Say what is happening just now.

At playtime –
Barbara **always plays** with Susan.
Ronny **sometimes plays** with them.
After school –
Ronny **often does** his homework with Kevin.
Barbara **never plays** with Susan because Susan lives in Escrick.

This morning they **are playing** hopscotch.
But **today** he **is playing** with Kevin.

Just now they **are doing** German.

But **this afternoon** Barbara **is sitting** in the school bus. She **is going** to Susan's house for tea.

Unit 6 Step 3

6 By bus, by train

What about you?
Say how you often/always/sometimes/never come to school.

7 What's the weather like?

11 o'clock is "playtime" in British schools. Every morning the children look out of the window.
"What's the weather like? Can we go out?"
"Yes, we can. It's warm./The sun is shining…"
"No, we can't. It's cold./It's raining…"

What's the weather like?

⟨8 Let's sing a song: The sun has got his hat on⟩

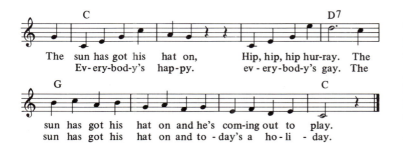

The sun has got his hat on,
Hip, hip, hip hurray.
The sun has got his hat on
And he's coming out to play.
Everybody's happy,
Everybody's gay.
The sun has got his hat on
And today's a holiday.

eighty-nine 89

Moorsrail

Unit 6
⟨ Authentic Britain: Moorsrail ⟩

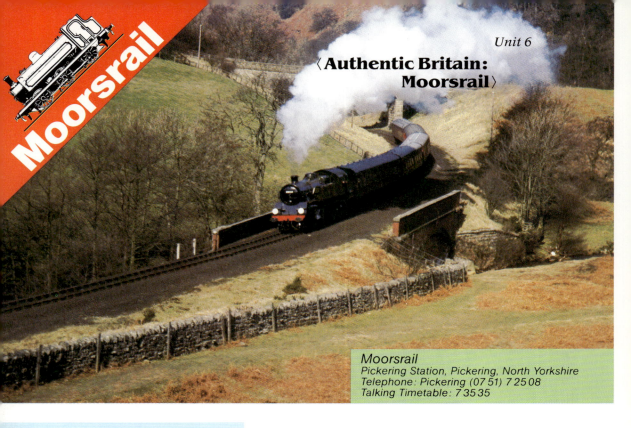

Moorsrail
Pickering Station, Pickering, North Yorkshire
Telephone: Pickering (0751) 72508
Talking Timetable: 73535

Tourist Information
The Tourist Information Centre at Pickering Station will help you find accom mod tell the Tel:

Ca
Pick
East
Goo
Nati
Gro
Nati

Co
Pick
Gro

Re
Ligh
Pickering, Goathland and Grosmont. Bar facilities on most trains.

Unit 7

Terraced houses in Worcester

Semi-detached houses in York

⟨Photo page:
Houses in Britain⟩

A detached house
in Guildford

Unit 7 Step 1

1 The 'Twenty Questions' game

Barbara and Ronny are playing 'Twenty Questions' with Kevin in his room.
Someone thinks of a thing, and the others must guess it.
They can only ask twenty questions, and the questions must always have 'yes' or 'no'
for an answer. Now it is Ronny's turn to think of something.

5 *Ronny:* O.K. I'm ready.
Barbara: Can I eat it?
Ronny: No, you can't.

Kevin: Is it useful?
Ronny: No, it isn't. Not really.

10 *Barbara:* Do I use it at school?
Ronny: No, you don't.
You don't use it at school.

Kevin: Do we use it every day?
Ronny: Well, I don't use it every day.
15 But perhaps you do.

Kevin: Do I use it at home?
Ronny: Yes, you do. Five questions gone.

Barbara: Can you buy it in a shop?
Ronny: Yes, you can.

20 *Barbara:* Do the Pearsons sell it in their shop?
Ronny: Yes, they do.

Kevin: Do I write with it? Or do I work with it?
Ronny: No, you don't.
You don't write with it,
25 and you don't work with it.

Kevin: This is difficult. Wait –
do I play with it?
Ronny: Good question.
Yes, you do.

30 *Kevin:* Do **you** play with it?
Ronny: No, I don't. Eleven questions gone!
Kevin: Let me think. Oh, no! Kate is coming upstairs.
Kate: Hands up! Hands up!
Kevin: Hey, come here, Kate! That's *my* water-pistol.
35 *Barbara:* Hey, Ronny! Is it a water-pistol?!
Ronny: Yes, it is.
Kevin: Hooray! We've got the answer, Barbara!
It's a water-pistol! Thanks, Kate.
Ronny: Oh, Kate! *Must* you come in just when I'm winning?

92 ninety-two

1 Questions and answers

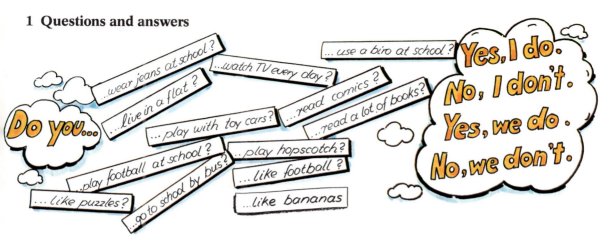

2 Timmy wants to know

Ronny is at home. He is looking after Timmy. Timmy is asking him a lot of questions.

Do

the Pearsons	read a lot of books?
teachers	like cats?
German children	go to school every afternoon?
dogs	sell toy cars?
cats	eat dog biscuits?
bus drivers	cry at night?
Kevin and Kate	use their water-pistols at school?
babies	wear uniform?

Yes, they do.
No, they don't.
No idea! Sorry!
Sometimes.

Timmy: Do German children go to school every afternoon?
Ronny: No, they don't.
Find Timmy's questions, and give Ronny's answers.
Can you think of more questions for Timmy?

3 Role Play Do you want a...

Unit 7 Step 2

2 All about Kevin

Colin, a boy in Kevin's school, is asking questions.

	Do you **live** in Fulford Road, Kevin?	No, I **don't**.
Where	do you **live**?	I **live** in Selby Road.
	Do your parents **open** the shop at 9 o'clock?	No, they **don't**.
When	do they **open** the shop?	They **open** it at 8 o'clock.
	Do they **sell** clothes?	No, they **don't**.
What	do they **sell**?	They **sell** newspapers and books.
	Do they **sell** a lot of newspapers?	Yes, they **do**.
How many	do they **sell** every day?	They **sell** nearly two hundred.
	Do you **like** Selby Road, Kevin?	Yes, I **do**.
Why	do you **like** it?	I **like** it because I've got good friends there.

1 ... and all about Colin

Now Kevin is asking Colin questions.

a) *Find the right questions and answers.*

Where   How   What   How many   When   When

... do you live?
... do you come to school?
... sandwiches do you bring to school?
... do you have tea?
... do you do your homework?
... do you do after tea?

At half past five.
Before tea.
In a flat in Station Road.
On my bike.
I play, or I read, or I watch TV.
I don't bring sandwiches, I bring an apple.

b) *Now ask your friends.*

2 Tell me ...

1. Do you live in Germany?
2. Where do you go to school?
3. Do you go to school on Saturdays?
4. How do you go home after school?
5. When do you get home after school?
6. Where do you do your homework?
7. Do you do your homework with your friend?
8. Do you like English?
9. What do you do in the afternoon?
10. Do you eat chocolate every day?
11. Do you like cats?
12. When do you go to bed?

Unit 7 Step 2

3 Breakfast

What do you usually have for breakfast, Barbara?

"I have a glass of milk, cornflakes with milk, an egg, and two pieces of bread and butter.

What do you usually have for breakfast, Ronny?

"I have bacon and egg, a piece of toast with marmalade, and a cup of tea."

What do you usually have for breakfast in Germany, Mr Klein?

I have two rolls with cheese or sausage, and two cups of coffee.

What do you have for breakfast?

4 Let's talk about breakfast

Talk about breakfast with your friends. Here are some ideas.

– Where do you have breakfast? (in the dining-room/kitchen/in bed!)
– When do you have breakfast on Mondays/Sundays?
– Do you have rolls or bread for breakfast?
– How many rolls/pieces of bread do you have?
– Do you have milk for breakfast?
– Do you like tea/coffee ...?

5 Role Play At the breakfast table

Your English friend is visiting you in Germany.
You are having breakfast.

Do you want a piece of bread or a roll?
Where's the marmalade?
Do you want another cup of tea?
This roll is good!
Can I have the toast, please?
More tea/toast/cornflakes ...?
Can you give me a cup of coffee, please?
What time is it?

A roll, please.
Here it is.
Yes, please/No, thank you.
Have another roll, then.
Here you are.
Yes, please/No, thank you.
Here you are/Sorry, it's all gone.
Oh dear, we're late for school.

ninety-five 95

Unit 7 Step 3

3 Upstairs and Downstairs

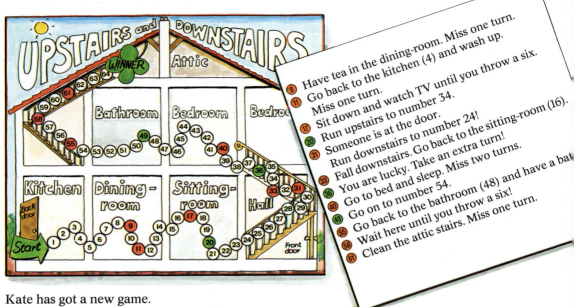

Kate has got a new game.

Kate: Let's play 'Upstairs and Downstairs'. Do you know the game, Barbara?
Barbara: No, I don't. Does Kevin know it?
Kate: No, he doesn't.
Kevin: O.K. Tell us how the game goes, Kate.
Kate: It's easy. Everyone gets a counter. You throw the dice, and you go through all the rooms in the house.
Barbara: Does the game start at the front door?
Kate: No, it doesn't. It starts at the back door. You go through the numbers, from 1 to 64.
Kevin: I see. When does the game end?
Kate: It ends when someone gets to the attic.
Barbara: O.K. Let's start. You throw first, Kate.
Kate: Six! That's good. I can go through the kitchen into the dining-room.
Kevin: Five!
Kate: You go to number 11. That's bad. Look, it's a red number.
Kevin: Red? Does that mean bad luck?

Kate: Yes, it does. Look: "Go back to the kitchen and wash up. Miss one turn."
Kevin: Ugh! Kate, your turn again.
Kate: Oh good! I've got a five. I'm on a green number now.
Barbara: What does that mean?
Kate: It means that you are lucky. "Run upstairs to number 34."
Kevin: You're always lucky!
Barbara: One. Oh no! "Someone is at the door. Run downstairs to number 24!"
Kevin: Bad luck, Barbara! My turn.
Kate: Wait – don't throw the dice.
Kevin: Why not?
Kate: Because you must miss a turn now.
Barbara: When does Kevin throw the dice again?
Kate: After you and me, of course.

Kate: Four! I'm in the attic. I'm the winner! Do you want to play again?
Kevin: No, we don't.
Barbara: No, not again, Kate!
Kate: Oh! Don't you like it? Why not?
Kevin: It's a silly game! That's why.

96 ninety-six

1 Comprehension Answer the questions.

a) 1. Do Kevin and Barbara know the game?
   2. Does the game start at the front door?
   3. Does a red number mean bad luck?
   4. Does the game end at the front door?
   5. Do Kevin and Barbara want to play again?

b) 1. What does Kate tell Kevin and Barbara?
   2. Where does the game start?
   3. What does a green number mean?
   4. Where does the game end?
   5. Why don't Kevin and Barbara want to play again?

2 Questions with 'do' and 'does'

a) *Put in 'do, don't, does, doesn't'.*
   1. *Ronny:* … you like lemonade?
      Barbara: Yes, I …
   2. *Helen:* … the Pearsons sell comics?
      Peter: Yes, they …
   3. *Elke:* … you all like milk?
      Kevin: No, we …
   4. *Barbara:* … Kevin read your books?
      Kate: No, he …
   5. *Ben:* … the train stop at Pickering?
      Peter: Yes, it …
   6. *Mrs Pearson:* … Barbara speak German to you?
      Mrs Klein: No, she … . She speaks English to me.

b)

Do	you your parents dogs	like	cats biscuits TV	Yes,	he she	does. doesn't.
Does	your brother/sister/friend …		cornflakes comics …	No,	I we they	do. don't.

Do you **like** milk chocolate, Ronny?   Yes, I **do**.
Do you **like** milk?   No, I **don't**. (I **don't like** milk.)
What **do** you drink then?   Water!
Do you all **play** with toys?   Yes, we **do**.
Do you **play** with Timmy's toys?   No, we **don't**. (We **don't play** with Timmy's toys.)
How often **do** you play together?   Every day.
Do the Pearsons **sell** water-pistols?   Yes, they **do**.
Do they **sell** biscuits?   No, they **don't**. (They **don't sell** biscuits.)
How many water-pistols **do** they sell a week?   Only two or three.
Does Kevin **use** his water-pistol at home?   Yes, he **does**.
Does Kate **use** it at school?   No, she **doesn't**. (She **doesn't use** it at school.)
Where **does** she use it?   Outside the shop.
Does the bus **get** to school at quarter to nine?   Yes, it **does**.
Does it **take** the children home again at twelve?   No, it **doesn't**. (It **doesn't take** them home again at twelve.)
When **does** it take them home?   At four o'clock.

3 Sundays at the Griffins' house

Say what Mrs Griffin and Sally do on Sundays. Start like this:
At 9 o'clock the Griffins have breakfast in the dining-room.
After breakfast ... At half past eleven Mrs Griffin always ... .

4 Susan's dog

a) Susan has got a dog. It's a very funny dog. It sleeps in Susan's

It drinks It eats and

It sleeps on Susan's It plays with

And it runs after

b) Jane is asking Barbara about Susan's dog.

Give Barbara's answers.

Example: "Does Susan's dog sleep in the kitchen?" "No, it doesn't sleep in the kitchen. It sleeps in her bedroom."

1. Does it drink water?
2. Does it eat dog biscuits?
3. Does it sleep on the floor?
4. Does it play with other dogs?
5. Does it run after sticks?

5 Let's play 'Twenty Questions'

You can play 'Twenty Questions' in class. One of you thinks of a thing, and the others must guess what it is. These questions are often useful:

Can you buy it in a shop?
Is it useful?
Do you use it at home/at school?
Can you play with it/eat it?

Is it big/small?
Do children use it?
Can you carry it?

Do you put things in it/on it?
Is it in the house?
Do you see it/use it outside?

Unit 7 Step 3

6 Barbara – and you

Example: **Does Barbara** live in a village? – No, **she doesn't. She lives** in a town.
Do you live in a village? – Yes, **I do.** (Yes, **we do.**)
No, **I don't.** (No, **we don't.**)
I/We don't live in a village. **I/We live** in …

7 Look, listen and say

[d] – [t]	ride, right, friend, front	Kate is riding her bike. David is with her. I can't understand Anne.
[g] – [k]	bag, back, dog, sock	There's a bag up in the attic. Jack's dog is big and black.
[b] – [p]	Webb, shop job, map	Wendy Webb is buying a map. Her sister has got a job in a shop.
[v] – [f]	twelve, half, live, scarf	It's half past twelve – I must go. I live in Fulford.

⟨8 Let's sing a song: If you're happy⟩

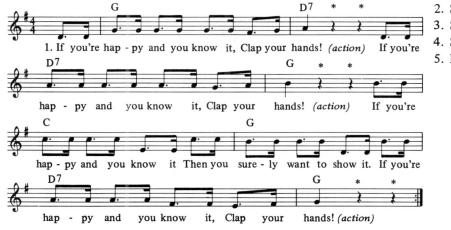

2. Stamp your feet!
3. Snap your fingers!
4. Say 'We are!'
5. Do all four!

1 **Circus in York**

What are they doing and what are they wearing?

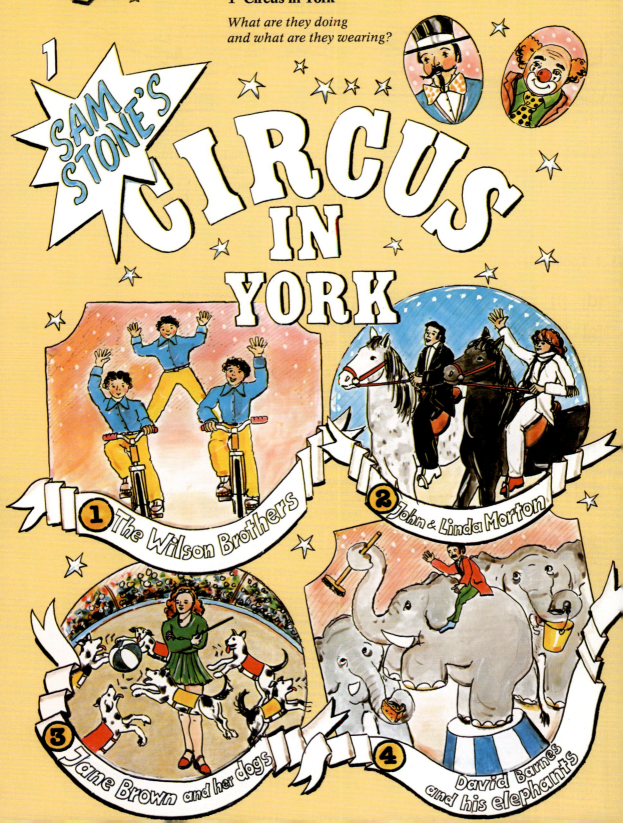

2 The hungry elephant

Here is a caravan at the circus. The elephant is looking for a packet of biscuits with its trunk. What a mess!

Where are the things in the caravan now?

Examples:
The radio is on the bed.
The apples are under the table.

Now you go on.

on behind under in in front of

3 What are these elephants doing?

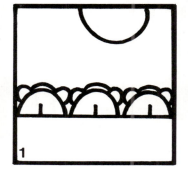
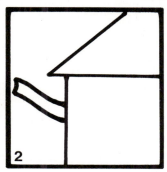
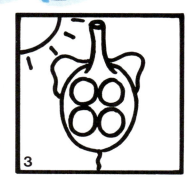

The elephants in picture 1 are … . *Go on.*

FUN PAGES 2

HOLIDAYS

1 On holiday

School is over for the four friends.
They are on holiday.

Ronny and his family
are staying at the seaside
for a week.

Kate and Kevin are staying
with their cousins
on a farm in Scotland.

Barbara is at home
for the first week
of the holidays.
Her mother has got
a new job. She helps
American tourists
and shows them round York.
Today Barbara is helping her.

102   *one hundred and two*

2 Role Play

You are on holiday and are talking to a British boy or girl.

You: Are you on holiday here?
British boy or girl: Yes, I am.
What about you?
Are you on holiday here?
You: Yes, I am.

British boy or girl: What's your name?
You: I'm …
What about you?
What's your name?
British boy or girl: My name is …

Now you go on. Here are some ideas.

3 A letter-puzzle

Kate and Kevin are making a letter-puzzle for Barbara.
Can you put the words in the right order and read the letter?

one hundred and three 103

3 GAMES, MAGIC and JOKES

1 How many?

Look at the picture and say how many things you can see. Work in groups. Help your group to be the winner.
Example: I can see … . There are … .   On the left/right there are … .

2 It's magic!

Here is a trick to show your friends.

Can you write a secret letter?

First take a piece of paper – perhaps a clean page from an old exercise book. The paper must be white. Now get some milk, and write your letter *with* the milk (use a clean pen for this). Be careful – don't use too much milk! Now, when the milk is dry, you can't see it, so nobody can read your letter. O.K. But how can your friend understand the secret letter? Easy. Your friend just holds the paper over a candle (but be careful that the paper doesn't get too warm!). When the paper is very warm, the milk starts to look brown, and your friend can soon read the letter!

3 A joke

Teacher: Now Tommy, I've got four apples in one hand and five in the other. What have I got?
Tommy: Big hands.

4🍎 + 5🍎 = ?

4 Kim's Game

In Britain children often play this game at birthday parties.
*Look at the picture for a minute. Then shut the book and write down what you can remember.
(There is a word for nearly every letter in the alphabet, but not for i, q, u, x, y and z.)*

5 The Magic Matchbox

Hold a matchbox – like this –
so your friends can see that it is empty.
Then put a small coin into the matchbox. Shut the matchbox, and say,
"Magic matchbox! Magic box! Give me two coins now!" Then open the box –
and there are two coins in it!
This is the trick. First put a small coin *under the matchbox lid*
(look at the picture!). Then push the box open (the coin
must be still under the lid). Now the box
looks empty. When you show the trick, shut
the box with your fingers over the end.
The secret coin falls into the box,
and you have got two coins in it!

6 A joke

Teacher : First I give you three rabbits and then I give you five rabbits. So how many rabbits have you got?
Susan : Nine.
Teacher : Nine?
Susan : Yes, I've got one rabbit at home.

one hundred and five 105

Additum Unit 5

1 Comprehension *Right or wrong?*   **ab Unit 5   Step 2**

1. A teacher from Fulford Comprehensive School is talking to Wendy Webb.
2. They are talking about Wendy's job.
3. Wendy is a taxi driver.
4. She collects the children from the villages.
5. Wendy must get up early.
6. They always get to school at quarter to eight.
7. In the afternoon Wendy can go home.

2 What the Pearsons do every day   **ab Unit 5   Step 3**

	I	come
	you	come
(Kevin)	he	
(Kate)	she }	comes
(the bus)	it	
	we	come
	you	come
	they	come

1. Mr and Mrs Pearson's day *starts* at quarter to six.
2. Mr Pearson ... to the station. He ... the newspapers.
3. At quarter past six the newspaper boys ... into the shop.
4. Mrs Pearson ... them their newspapers.
5. The boys ... them to the houses in Fulford.
6. "We always ... the shop at 8 o'clock," ... Mr Pearson.
7. Children often ... into the shop after school.
8. They ... pens, pencils and comics.

3 Wendy's day   **ab Unit 5   Step 3**

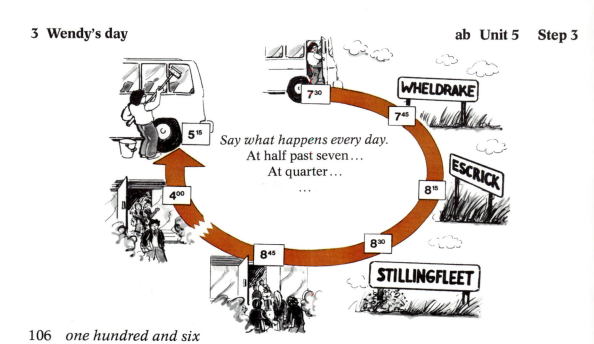

Say what happens every day.
At half past seven...
At quarter...
...

106   one hundred and six

Additum Unit 5

4 A day with Bonzo

ab Unit 5   Step 4

Look at the pictures and tell the story.

At quarter past 7   Then …   After that …   At ten o'clock …
Bonzo…

After the walk …   Then …   At 4 o'clock in the   In the evening …
                                afternoon …

5 It's Friday at the Bennetts' house

ab Unit 5   Step 4

Put in the right verb in the right form.

1. First Mr and Mrs Bennett … breakfast,
   and Ronny … his little brother.
2. Then they all … breakfast together.
3. At quarter past eight Ronny … to school.
4. Mrs Bennett … away in her taxi,
   and Mr Bennett … the telephone.
5. In the afternoon Mrs Bennett … home,
   and Mr and Mrs Bennett … with Timmy.
6. Then Mr Bennett … away in his taxi. He …
   his first passenger to the station.
7. At four o'clock Ronny … home from school,
   and Mrs Bennett and Ronny … Timmy for
   a walk.

one hundred and seven 107

Additum Unit 5

6 The mysterious piano player

ab Unit 5   Step 4

Anne Carson likes music.
She has piano lessons at school but the Carsons haven't got a piano at home yet. A neighbour has got an old piano and says that Anne can have it. The keys are yellow and there is no lid, but it is still a good piano. One day Mr Carson and three neighbours take the piano to the Carsons' house. Now Anne is very happy. Anne's baby sister Jane likes the piano, too, because she can make a lot of noise on it. In the evening Mr and Mrs Carson are out. Little Jane wants to play the piano, but Anne says, "No, Jane. You must go to bed now."

So Jane goes to bed. Then Anne does her homework. At nine o'clock she goes to bed, too. But what is that? She sits up in bed and listens. It is her
15 piano. She can hear music. – Well, not music, a lot of noise! Jane! Anne jumps out of bed, runs downstairs and switches on the light in the sitting-room. But there is nobody there. "Jane, come here! I know you're there!" she shouts. But there is no answer. Is it a trick? Anne switches off the light and goes upstairs to Jane's room. Jane is in bed. She is asleep.
20 Then Anne hears the piano again! Who can it be? Are her parents back? She runs downstairs and shouts, "Are you there, Mum and Dad?" She switches on the light in the sitting-room. But there is nobody there. And there is nobody in her parents' room and nobody in the kitchen. Now Anne is afraid. There is somebody downstairs at her piano!
25 It isn't her sister and it isn't her father or her mother. What can she do? There is no telephone in the house. Then she has an idea. She switches off all the lights and waits behind the open sitting-room door.
The sitting-room is dark, and there is no noise. Suddenly Anne hears the mysterious piano player again. She switches on the light and looks into the room. It is Puddles, the family cat, on the piano keys.

Right or wrong?
1. Anne has piano lessons at home.
2. Anne's sister is happy because she can have the piano.
3. Jane says, "You must go to bed now, Anne."
4. Anne plays the piano, then she does her homework.
5. Anne switches on the light in the bathroom.
6. At nine o'clock Jane is asleep.
7. Mr and Mrs Carson are in the kitchen.
8. The Carsons haven't got a telephone.
9. The sitting-room is dark but Anne can see the piano player.
10. Anne switches on the light and sees Puddles under the piano.

Additum Unit 5

7 The clown in the box   ab Unit 5   Step 4

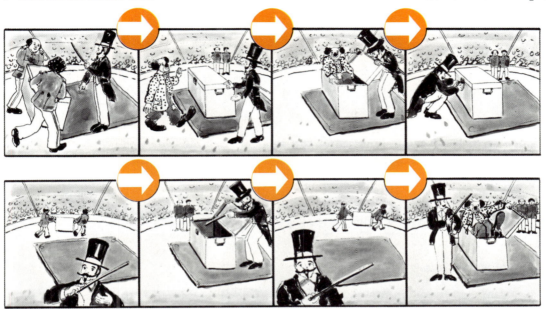

Look at the pictures and tell the story. Here are some words to help you: to open, to come in, to go, to put down, to lock, to sit down, to pick up, to show, to carry.

8 A letter from Barbara   ab Unit 5   Step 4

> 15 Selby Road
> Fulford
> YO5 4BD
>
> Dear class 6a,
> I'm in England now, so this letter is in English. We live in a big house in Selby Road. I like it here because I've got some new friends – Kate, Kevin and Ronny. On Saturdays we play together.
> I like the English breakfast – I always eat cornflakes with a lot of milk! The milkman comes with the milk every morning at 7 o'clock and puts the bottles in front of the door. This usually wakes me up!
> I leave the house at half past eight. We have lunch at school. Then there's school in the afternoon and we go home at 4 o'clock. I do my homework after school and then I usually go to Kate's house.
> I sometimes watch TV in the evenings, too.
>   Love from Barbara

Now tell your friends what Barbara writes in her letter. Start like this: She's in England now …

9 Listening comprehension: Ralph and his dog   ab Unit 5   Step 4

Barbara tells this story to Timmy. *Listen and answer the questions.*
[*New words:* to fetch = holen; what happens? = was passiert? second = zweiter; third = dritter]

1. What is the dog's name – Barker, Baker or Parker?
2. Why has he got this name?
3. Can he do a lot of tricks?
4. What must he do when Ralph throws the ball?
5. What happens when Ralph throws the ball the first time?
6. What happens when Ralph throws the ball the second time?
7. Why is Ralph angry?
8. Say what the dog does when Ralph throws the ball the third time.
9. Can Ralph find his dog?
10. Say what he does then.
11. Where is the dog?

one hundred and nine 109

Additum Unit 6

1 On time   ab Unit 6   Step 1

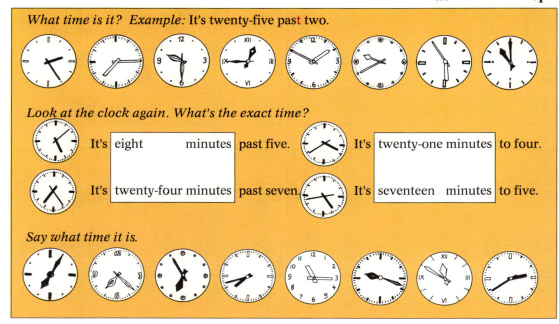

2 How they get to school every morning   ab Unit 6   Step 1

a) 1. Jenny goes to school by bus.
    2. Ben ...
    3. David ...
    4. Mr Jackson ...
    5. Helen is always late. She ...
    6. Mrs Griffin ...
    7. Sometimes Ronny is late in the morning. Then he ...
    8. Nobody ... to school ...

b) 1. She gets to school at seventeen minutes to nine.
    2. ...
    3. ...
    4. His train arrives at the station ...
    5. ...
    6. ...
    7. ...

Additum Unit 6

3 Timetables   ab Unit 6   Step 1

a) In timetables you often see this:

| 6.47 | 2.30 | 4.15 | 5.27 | 9.08 |

Then you can say: "six forty-seven"
"two thirty"   "four fifteen"
"five twenty-seven"   "nine oh eight"

b) *Here is the timetable for the morning train from Pickering to Grosmont.*

Pickering	leaves	10.25	11.25
Levisham	arrives	10.41	11.41
Levisham	leaves	10.44	11.44
Goathland	arrives	11.11	12.11
Goathland	leaves	11.20	12.20
Grosmont	arrives	11.30	12.30

A train leaves Pickering at ten twenty-five.
It arrives at Levisham at ten forty-one.
It leaves Levisham at …

Now you go on.

4 Early, late, on time   ab Unit 6   Step 1

a) *Look at the pictures.*
It's eleven twenty-five.
A train **is arriving** at Grosmont.
(A train is leaving …)
…

b) *Now look at the timetable.*
The train usually **arrives** at
Grosmont at eleven thirty.
(It usually leaves …)

5 Say what you do   ab Unit 6   Step 3

*Tell your friend what you always/usually/often/sometimes/never do.
Watch the word order!*

I { always / usually / often / sometimes / never }
- have breakfast at seven o'clock.
- eat cornflakes for breakfast.
- ride to school on my bike.
- go to school on Saturday morning.
- read comics.
- play cards with my friends.
- do my homework in the evening.

Go on.

one hundred and eleven   111

Additum Unit 6

6 After school ab Unit 6 Step 3

"Hello, Kevin. I'm writing a book for German school children. Tell them what you do after school."

"Well, I leave school at 4 o'clock. I get home at ten minutes past four. I go into the shop and say hello to my parents. Then I go upstairs. I take off my school uniform and put on jeans and a pullover. I usually help my parents in the shop for an hour. I fetch things from upstairs or carry things from the van into the shop. I have tea at six o'clock. Then I do my homework and watch TV a bit."

Now you *say what Kevin does after school.* He leaves school …

7 Making plans ab Unit 6 Step 3

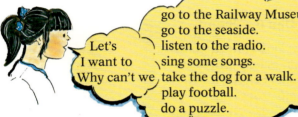 

Let's / I want to / Why can't we
- go to the Railway Museum.
- go to the seaside.
- listen to the radio.
- sing some songs.
- take the dog for a walk.
- play football.
- do a puzzle.

- Oh no, that's not a good idea.
- Oh no, not again!
- Sorry, I can't. I'm doing my homework.
- That's a good/great idea. Good, then I can … .

a) *Make plans with your neighbour.*

b) *Can you make five plans for this afternoon?*

8 Fizz ab Unit 6 Step 3

"Let's play 'fizz'," says Kevin. "I can't play that," says Barbara.
"Well, listen to us first," says Ronny. "Fizz is three."

Ronny: One	Kate: Wrong!	Ronny: Fizz	Kevin: You're out, Ronny.
Kate: Two	Two threes make six,	Kate: Ten	Thirteen has got
Kevin: Fizz	so six is 'fizz', too.	Ronny: Eleven	a three in it.
Ronny: Four	You're out.	Kate: Fizz	Barbara: Oh, I understand now.
Kate: Five	Ronny: Seven	Ronny: Thirteen	Let's start again.
Kevin: Six	Kate: Eight		

Can you *play 'fizz'?*

9 Who? ab Unit 6 Step 3

Answer these questions about the friends in Selby Road.
Examples:
"Who hasn't got a brother?" "Barbara hasn't." "Who has got a taxi?" "The Bennetts have."

1. Who can play hopscotch?
2. Who has got a sister?
3. Who must go to bed early in the evening?
4. Who can speak English and German?
5. Who has got a baby brother?
6. Who must go to Whitby with the friends?
7. Who can't go to Whitby?
8. Who has got a shop?
9. Who is ten years old?
10. Who can't play Fizz?

Additum Unit 6

10 On the beach
ab Unit 6　　Step 3

a) *Ask questions and give the answers.*

Is Kate …?
Are Ronny and Kevin …?
Has … **got** …?
Can …?

Who …?
Where …?
What is/are … **doing**?
How many …?

b) Say what people do on the beach.

Examples: People sometimes take their dogs for a walk on the beach.
People never eat cornflakes on the beach.

11 Listening comprehension: Seaside Special at Scarborough　　ab Unit 6　　Step 3

Today Seaside Special is at Scarborough [ˈskɑːbərə]
[*new: to live* = leben, wohnen]

Listen, and then answer the questions.

1. What is the weather like?
2. Are there a lot of people at the beach?
3. Who is talking to the man on the radio?
4. Where is she from?
5. Why is she lucky?
6. What happens when the sun is shining?
7. When is the beach empty?
8. What can you do then?
9. What is the girl's request?
10. And who is it for?

Additum Unit 6

12 In the snack-bar   ab Unit 6   Step 3

There is a small snack-bar near the beach. There aren't many people in it.

The door opens and a boy and a girl come in.

First they take a tray and put a piece of cake and a yoghurt on it.

Then the girl takes a glass of lemonade, and the boy takes a glass of milk.

Then they pay at the cash desk.

After that they look for an empty table.

Then they sit down and begin to eat and drink.

They look through the window at the people on the beach.

Then the door opens and a mother and her child come in …

Then three boys come in …

Then an old man comes in …

13 All about me   ab Unit 6   Step 3

Talk about yourself. Here are some ideas.
My name is …
I am … years old.
I've got … brothers/sisters.
I haven't got brothers or sisters.
I come from …
My address is …
My telephone number is …

I go to … school. I'm in class …
My teacher's name is …

I get up at …
I walk to school./I go to school by …
I get to school at …
I usually get home at …

In the afternoon I …
and in the evening I …

On Sundays I …

I can/can't play the piano/swim.

114   *one hundred and fourteen*

Additum Unit 7

1 Elke and Jane   ab Unit 7   Step 1

a) Jane is a new girl in Elke's class. The two girls sit together. After school, Jane asks Elke a lot of questions.

Do you live in Heslington?	No, I don't. I live in Fulford, in Selby Road.
… go to school by bus?	No, … … on my bike.
… come from here?	No, … . … Germany.
Oh! … speak German?	Yes, … . My father is German, but my mother is English.
I see. … like school here?	Yes, … . But I … like school uniform!

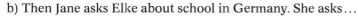

b) Then Jane asks Elke about school in Germany. She asks…

1. … if German school children wear uniform.
2. … if they go to school on Saturdays.
3. … if they have lunch at school.
4. … if they go to school every afternoon.
5. … if they get homework every day.
6. … if they start school at nine o'clock.

Now ask Jane's questions, and give Elke's answers.

2 Role Play Different plans   ab Unit 7   Step 2

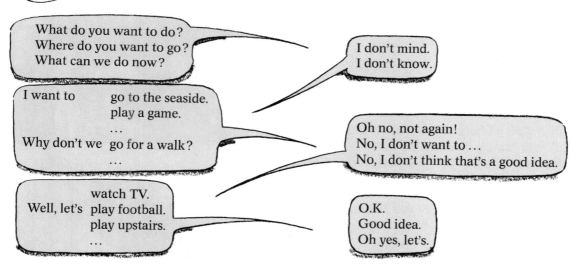

What do you want to do?
Where do you want to go?
What can we do now?

I don't mind.
I don't know.

I want to   go to the seaside.
            play a game.
            …
Why don't we go for a walk?
              …

Oh no, not again!
No, I don't want to …
No, I don't think that's a good idea.

           watch TV.
Well, let's play football.
           play upstairs.
           …

O.K.
Good idea.
Oh yes, let's.

You play the roles. Here is an example:

Ronny: What do you want to do now?
Barbara: I don't mind.
Kate: Why don't we go for a walk?
Kevin: No, I don't want to go for a walk.
Barbara: Well, let's play upstairs.
Ronny: Oh yes, let's.

Additum Unit 7

3 Sunday afternoon out   ab Unit 7   Step 3

"Have a good time at the museum, and don't forget
to look after Timmy!" says Mr Bennett.
"Mum and I are out until five or half past,
so you can have a nice long afternoon out together."
5   "O.K., Dad. Goodbye!" calls Ronny.
He and Timmy go to the bus stop with Kate, Kevin and
Barbara. They take a bus to the Castle Museum.
They get there at half past two.

The Castle Museum is very interesting,
10 and a lot of other children are there, too.
There is an old street in the museum,
with old houses and shops.
Timmy does not want to leave the old sweet shop.
He thinks it is so wonderful!
15 At four o'clock they go. Timmy wants to walk back,
but it is too far, so they take a bus again.

On the way Kevin looks out of the window.
"Look!" he says, "there's David on his new bike!"
David is in their class at school.
20 "Let's get off here and say hello!" shouts Ronny.
"We're coming to a bus stop now."
So they all leave their seats and get off when the bus stops.
David sees his friends at the bus stop and rides over to them.
"That's a nice bike!" says Barbara.
25 "Can I ride it a minute?" asks Ronny. "Thanks, David!"
"Then it's my turn," says Kate. "O.K., David?"

At last they say goodbye to David and he rides home.
"We can walk back home from here," says Kevin.
"But wait," says Ronny. "Where's Timmy?"
30 Timmy is not there. They look up and down the road,
and they call, but he does not come.
"Why doesn't he answer?" says Ronny.

116   *one hundred and sixteen*

Additum Unit 7

"Perhaps he's on his way back to the museum," says Barbara.
"You know, to that old sweet shop."
35 "Don't be silly," says Kevin. "It's too far."
"The river!" says Ronny. "There's a road down to the river over there. Dad and I sometimes go for a walk with him there."
"Let's look there, then!" says Kate.
They run down to the river, but they do not find Timmy.
40 Ronny is very unhappy and starts to cry.
"What can we do?" he says.
"Don't cry," says Kate. She looks at her watch.
"Why don't we go home? It's five to five.
Perhaps your mum and dad are back now, Ronny."

45 At ten past five the four friends get back again.
They are all unhappy and afraid. Ronny is crying again.
He does not want to tell his parents.
"It's the only way," says Kevin. "Tell your mum and dad, and they can telephone the police."
50 "You must all come with me, then," says Ronny. "Please!"
"Look, your dad is arriving in his taxi now!" says Barbara.

They run to the taxi and Mr Bennett opens the window.
"Hey, what's all this? Why are you crying, Ronny?"
"We must ring up the police," cries Ronny.
55 "Timmy is gone! We don't know where he is."
"What?!" says Mr Bennett.
"Come in with me, all of you, and tell me all about it."
They all go round the house to the back door.
And what do they hear?
60 A small voice. Someone is singing.
"Timmy!"
Timmy is sitting on the back doorstep.
He does not look unhappy at all.
"Hello," he says. "I'm the winner. I'm back home first!"

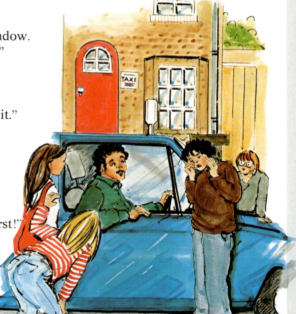

one hundred and seventeen 117

Additum Unit 7

4 Comprehension   *Answer the questions.*   ab Unit 7   Step 3

1. Where do the children go on Sunday afternoon? How do they get there?
2. What does Timmy like at the museum?
3. Why don't they walk back home?
4. What do they do when they see David on his bike?
5. Do they all find the bike interesting? What about Timmy?
6. Why does Timmy go home alone?
7. Why do Ronny and the others go down to the river?
8. Why does Ronny start to cry?
9. When do the children get back home? What do they want to do then?
10. What does Mr Bennett say when Ronny tells him about Timmy?
11. Where is Timmy sitting when the others get home? What is he doing? Why?

5 In the house   ab Unit 7   Step 3

What are Kate and Kevin doing? And where? What does Mrs Pearson say?
Example: Kate is doing her homework in the kitchen.
            Mrs Pearson: Don't do your homework in the kitchen, Kate.
                             Go into your bedroom and do it there.

 6 Listening comprehension: Standing at the bus stop   ab Unit 7   Step 3

Listen to the cassette and answer the questions.
1. Where does the first boy want to go?
2. How long must he wait?
3. Does the second boy live in York?
4. What is the boy from Newcastle doing in Escrick?
5. How does the boy from Escrick know Newcastle?
6. What does he think of Newcastle?
7. And what does the boy from Newcastle say about York?
8. What does the boy from Escrick do in the evenings? Where? And when?
9. What is there the next day?
10. Where is Kenton?

118   *one hundred and eighteen*

Grammar

Alphabetisches Verzeichnis der grammatischen Ausdrücke

In der Grammatik kommen immer wieder Ausdrücke vor, wie zum Beispiel Infinitiv oder Hilfsverb. Wenn man jetzt nicht genau weiß, was damit gemeint ist, oder wenn man es wieder vergessen hat, kann man in dieser Liste nachsehen. Sie enthält die wichtigsten Ausdrücke, die in der Grammatik verwendet werden.

Lateinisch	Deutsch	Englisch	Englisches Beispiel
Adjektiv	Eigenschaftswort	adjective	Kate is **ill**.
Adverb	Umstandswort	adverb	Kevin **often** helps his father.
adverbiale Bestimmung des Orts und der Zeit	Orts- und Zeitbestimmung (Umstandsbestimmung des Orts und der Zeit)	adverb of place and time	**in the park** **in the morning**
Artikel		article	
bestimmter Artikel		definite article	**the** [ðə /ðiː]
unbestimmter Artikel		indefinite article	**a, an**
Genitiv	Wesfall	genitive	Timm**y's** toys
Hilfsverb	Hilfszeitwort	auxiliary verb	I **can** speak English.
Imperativ	Befehlsform	imperative	**Go** to bed soon, Ronny.
Infinitiv	Grundform	infinitive	**to go**
Kardinalzahlen	Grundzahlen	cardinal numbers	**one, two**
Konsonant	Mitlaut	consonant	**g, t**
	Mengenangabe	expression of quantity	**a pound of** butter
Objekt			
direktes Objekt	Satzergänzung	direct object	I can see **a box**.
indirektes Objekt	indirekte Satzergänzung.	indirect object	Give **the dog** a biscuit.
Personalpronomen	persönliches Fürwort	personal pronoun	**she, him**
Plural	Mehrzahl	plural	the girl**s**
Possessivpronomen	besitzanzeigendes Fürwort	possessive adjective	**his, her, my**
Präposition	Verhältniswort	preposition	**in** the van
Präsens	Gegenwart	present	
einfaches Präsens	einfache Zeitform der Gegenwart	simple present	I **get up** at seven o'clock.
Verlaufsform des Präsens		present progressive	We're **playing** cards.
Singular	Einzahl	singular	**a boy**
Subjekt	Satzgegenstand	subject	**Timmy** is in bed.
Substantiv	Hauptwort	noun	**van**
Verb	Tätigkeitswort	verb	**to run**
Vokal	Selbstlaut	vowel	**a, e, i, o, u**

First Scenes

§1 Lang- und Kurzformen von 'to be'   Long and short forms of 'to be'

To be ist ein Verb, das in verschiedenen Formen auftritt. Die Verbform, vor der *to* steht, nennt man Infinitiv (Grundform). *To be* ist also eine Infinitivform. Die folgenden Sätze enthalten weitere Formen von *to be*.

Langform	
I am	new.
You are	late.
He is	ill.
She is	ill, too.
It is	nine o'clock.
We are	from Leeds.
You are	late, Kevin and Ronny.
They are	from York.

Kurzform	
I'm	new.
You're	late.
He's	ill.
She's	ill, too.
It's	nine o'clock.
We're	from Leeds.
You're	late, Kevin and Ronny.
They're	from York.

- Verbformen von *to be* können in Langform oder Kurzform auftreten.
- Bei der Kurzform werden weggelassene Buchstaben durch einen Apostroph = Auslassungsstrich (') ersetzt.

Beim Sprechen verwendet man meist die Kurzform, beim Schreiben die Langform. Wenn man ein Gespräch aufschreibt, verwendet man meistens die Kurzform.

§2 Die Personalpronomen (persönliche Fürwörter)   Personal pronouns

I, you, he, she, it – we, you, they: Das sind Personalpronomen. Auf deutsch:
ich, du, er, sie, es – wir, ihr, sie.
Personalpronomen stehen für Personen, sie heißen daher im Deutschen auch persönliche Fürwörter. Obwohl *it* immer für Sachen steht, gehört es auch dazu.

Beim Gebrauch der Personalpronomen muß man folgende Dinge beachten:

Are	you	from York, Ronny?
Bist	du	aus York,
Are	you	Kevin and Kate?
Seid	ihr	
Are	you	Mrs Griffin?
Sind	Sie	

How old is Kevin?	He	's eleven.
…Kate?	She	's ten.

- *You* kann *du*, *ihr* oder *Sie* heißen.

- *He* steht für eine männliche Person (Kevin, Ronny…).
  She steht für eine weibliche Person (Kate, Mrs Griffin…).

 weist auf Dinge hin, die besonders beachtet werden müssen.

First Scenes

Here is the bucket.	It 's clean.
…der Eimer.	Er ist sauber.
There is the door.	It 's dirty.
…die Tür.	Sie ist schmutzig.
This is the house.	It 's empty.
…das Haus.	Es ist leer.
Where is the cat?	It 's over there.
…die Katze?	Sie ist dort drüben.

- Im Gegensatz zum Deutschen steht für eine Sache immer *it*.

- Auch für Tiere verwendet man gewöhnlich *it*.

 Für Tiere, deren Namen man kennt, verwendet man *he* oder *she*:
z. B. Lassie is my dog. **She's** a good dog.
Toby is Anne's dog, too. **He's** terrible.

§3 Die Verneinung von 'to be'
The negative of 'to be'

Singular (Einzahl)			**Plural** (Mehrzahl)		
	I'm not	ill.	We	aren't	in the van.
	You aren't	late, Kevin.	You	aren't	late, Kevin and Kate.
Mr Pearson	isn't	a teacher.			
Mrs Bennet	isn't	in the shop.	They	aren't	from York.
The box	isn't	empty.			

- Man verneint *to be*, indem man den Formen von *to be* **not** hinzufügt: *I am not…, you are not…, he is not* usw. In der gesprochenen Sprache wird
I am not zu **I'm not** verkürzt,
are not zu **aren't**
is not zu **isn't** zusammengezogen.

§4 Fragen und Kurzantworten mit 'to be'
Questions and answers with 'to be'

Are you from Germany?	Yes, I am.	Ja.
Is Ronny from York?	Yes, he is.	Ja.
Is Kate from York?	No, she isn't.	Nein.
Is your shop in Selby Road?	Yes, it is.	Ja.
Kevin and Kate, **are you** from York?	No, we aren't.	Nein.

⚠ Bei Kurzantworten mit *yes* benützt man immer die Langformen von *to be*, z. B. *Yes, she is*.

- *yes* oder *no* allein kommt als Antwort im Englischen auch vor. Meistens antwortet man aber mit einem verkürzten Satz, einer sogenannten Kurzantwort.

 Auf die Frage *Is that…?* antwortet man *Yes, it is./No, it isn't*, auch wenn nach Personen gefragt wird: z. B. **Is that** Mrs Pearson? – Yes, **it** is.

First Scenes

§5 Die Possessivpronomen (besitzanzeigende Fürwörter)
The possessive adjectives

I'm not Ronny.	**My**	name is Kevin.
You're in 1 B.	**Your**	teacher is Mrs Griffin.
He's from Leeds.	**His**	name is Ben.
She's a teacher.	**Her**	name is Mrs Barnes.
We're from York.	**Our**	flat is in Selby Road.
You're late, Kevin and Ronny.	**Your**	friends are here.
They're from Germany.	**Their**	house is in Selby Road, too.

- Die Possessivpronomen zeigen, zu wem jemand oder etwas gehört.
  Z.B.: *my* verwendest du, wenn etwas dir gehört.
  his verwendest du, wenn etwas einem Jungen oder einem Mann gehört.

- *Your* kann *dein, euer* oder *Ihr* heißen. Z.B. Is that **your** dog? Ist das dein/euer/Ihr Hund?
  (Vgl. §2: *you = du, ihr* oder *Sie*)

 Die Formen *your* (dein, euer, Ihr) und *you're* (du bist, ihr seid, Sie sind) sind leicht zu verwechseln, weil sie gleich gesprochen werden. Beim Schreiben muß man genau aufpassen, welche Form gemeint ist.

§6 s-Genitiv
s-genitive

Timmy is Ronny	**'s**	brother.	Timmy ist Ronnys	Bruder.
Kate is Kevin	**'s**	sister.	Kate ist Kevins	Schwester.
Is that Mr Pearson	**'s**	taxi?	Ist das Herrn Pearsons	Taxi?
No, it is Mrs Bennett	**'s**	taxi.	Nein, es ist Frau Bennetts	Taxi.

- Der s-Genitiv zeigt an, zu wem jemand oder etwas gehört. Anders als im Deutschen steht im Englischen ein Apostroph (') vor dem Genitiv-*s*.

§7 Have got/has got

I have got	a new friend	Ich habe einen neuen Freund.
You have got	a baby brother!	Du hast einen kleinen Bruder!
He **has** got	a teddy.	Er hat einen Teddy.
She **has** got	a new cupboard.	Sie hat einen neuen Schrank.
It **has** got	two doors.	Er hat zwei Türen.
We have got	a dog.	Wir haben einen Hund.
You have got	our books.	Ihr habt unsere Bücher.
They have got	a new flat.	Sie haben eine neue Wohnung.

- Man gebraucht *have got/has got* im Sinne von *etwas haben/besitzen*.

First Scenes

§8 Die Verneinung von 'have got/has got'
The negative of 'have got/has got'

I haven't got	a car.	We haven't got	a new van.
Ich habe kein	Auto.	Wir haben keinen	neuen Lieferwagen.
You haven't got	my name in the register.	You haven't got	your books.
She hasn't got	a sponge.		Ihr habt eure Bücher nicht.
		They haven't got	a cat.

- In der Verneinung tritt *not* zwischen die Formen *have/has* und *got*; *have not* und *has not* werden in der gesprochenen Sprache zu *haven't* und *hasn't* zusammengezogen (vgl. §3).

§9 Fragen und Kurzantworten mit 'have got/has got'
Questions and short answers with 'have got/has got'

Kevin,	have	you	got	the bucket?	Yes,	I have.	Ja.
Kate,	have	you	got	the sponge?	No,	I haven't.	Nein.
	Has	dad	got	a box?	Yes,	he has.	Ja.
	Has	he	got	the brush?	No,	he hasn't.	Nein.
	Has	Mum	got	my water-pistol?	No,	she hasn't.	Nein.
	Have	the Pearsons got		a taxi?	No, they haven't.		Nein.

- Bei der Kurzantwort läßt man *got* weg. Zur Verwendung von Kurzantworten vgl. §4.

§10 Die Fragewörter 'where, who, what'
The question words 'where, who, what'

Where	are you, Kevin?		I'm in the shop.
Where	is your dad?	**Wo?**	He's out.
Where	is Kate?		She's on the van.
Where	are you	from?	**Woher?**	I'm from Leeds.
Where	are they	from?		They're from York.
What	is that?		It's Timmy's taxi.
What	is in the bucket?	**Was?**	There is water in the bucket.
What	has Kevin got?		He has got a water-pistol.
What	has Mrs Bennett got?		She has got a new pullover.
Who	is that?	**Wer?**	It's my English teacher.
Who	is your English teacher?		Her name is Mrs Griffin.

Englisch	where [weə]	who [huː]
Deutsch	wo	wer

Unit 1

§11 Zusammenstellung der Kurzformen (Scenes 1–9) Unit 1 Steps 1/2

Kurzformen von 'to be'			Kurzformen mit 'not'		
I	'm	Kevin Pearson.	I	'm not	Ronny Bennett.
You	're	new.	You	aren't	in 5 a.
He	's	my father.	He	isn't	at home.
She	's	a taxi driver.	She	isn't	my teacher.
It	's	Saturday morning.	It	isn't	raining.
We	're	from Leeds.	We	aren't	from York.
You	're	lucky, boys.	You	aren't	late.
They	're	in the flat.	They	aren't	in the shop.

Where	's	Mr Bennett from?	I	haven't	got your book.
Where	's	my pencil?	He	hasn't	got a car.
What	's	on the table?	We	haven't	got a dog.
Who	's	Kevin's father?			
There	's	a book in the box.	I	can't	speak Danish.
That	's	great.	They	can't	help us.

Let's… ist die Kurzform von *Let us…* und enthält keine Form von *to be!*
Z. B. Let's play cards.
Laß(t) uns Karten spielen.

§12 Das Hilfsverb 'can' Unit 1 Step 2
The auxiliary verb 'can'

I	can	speak	English.		
Barbara	can	speak	German and English.		
I	can't (cannot)	play	hopscotch.		
Timmy	can't (cannot)	carry	a bucket.		
	Can	you	speak	English?	Yes, I can.
	Can	Ronny	drive	a taxi?	No, he can't.
	Can	they	speak	German?	No, they can't.

- Das Hilfsverb *can* lautet in allen Personen gleich.

- Die verneinte Form von *can* heißt *cannot* ['kænɒt]. Meistens wird beim Sprechen – häufig auch beim Schreiben – die Kurzform *can't* [kɑːnt] verwendet.

124 one hundred and twenty-four

13 This/that

Unit 1 Step 3

Diese beiden Wörter gebraucht man, wenn man auf **eine** Person oder **einen** Gegenstand zeigt.

- Wenn zwei Personen oder Dinge gegenübergestellt werden, sagt man **zuerst** *this*, **dann** *that*.

- *This* gebraucht man auch, wenn man auf etwas zeigt, das ganz nahe ist.
  That gebraucht man, wenn man auf etwas zeigt, das weiter entfernt ist.

Unit 2

§14 Die Verlaufsform (Gegenwart)
The present progressive

Unit 2 Steps 3/4

a) Mrs Bennett is **clean**ing the car.	Frau Bennett ist (gerade) dabei, das Auto zu waschen.
Kevin **is help**ing his father.	Kevin hilft (im Moment) seinem Vater.
Ronny **is carry**ing a bucket.	Ronny trägt (gerade) einen Eimer.
Barbara and Kate **are watch**ing Timmy.	Barbara und Kate sehen (gerade) Timmy zu.
"What **are** you do**ing**, Timmy?"	„Was machst du (gerade), Timmy?"
"**I'm driv**ing my taxi."	„Ich fahre (gerade) in meinem Taxi."

- Mit dieser Verlaufsform wird ein Vorgang beschrieben, der noch nicht zu Ende ist. Diese Form drückt auch aus, daß jemand gerade dabei ist, etwas zu tun.
- Sie wird gebildet mit einer Form von *to be: am/are/is/are* und dem Infinitiv des Verbs + ing-Endung:

I	+	am	+	go - ing
She	+	is	+	read - ing

(handelnde Person) + (passende Form) + (Tätigkeitswort + ing)
                   von *to be*)

 Im Deutschen kennt man die Verlaufsform nicht; die Bedeutung dieser Form wird oft mit **gerade, im Moment, jetzt usw.** ausgedrückt.

b) "**Are** you read**ing** a comic, Ronny?"	"No, **I'm not**."
"**Is** Timmy watch**ing** TV?"	"No, **he isn't**."
"What **are** you do**ing**, then?"	"**I'm not** read**ing** comics, and Timmy **isn't** watch**ing** TV. We**'re** play**ing** with Timmy's cars."

§15 Die Schreibung der Verben in der Verlaufsform

clean carry help		Kate is Ronny is Kevin is	**clean**ing **carry**ing **help**ing	the car. three books. his father.
drive shine	ℯ̸ ℯ̸	Dad is The sun is	**driv**ing **shin**ing.	the taxi.
sit run	+t +n	Timmy is Barbara is	**sitt**ing **runn**ing	in the box. into the shop.

- Bei den meisten Verben wird die *ing*-Endung einfach an den Infinitiv angehängt.
- Verben mit stummem *-e* am Ende verlieren dieses *-e* vor der *ing*-Endung.
- Verben mit einem kurzen Vokal vor dem Endkonsonanten verdoppeln diesen Endkonsonanten.

Unit 3

16 Das Hilfsverb 'must'   The auxiliary verb 'must'   Unit 3 Step 1

The girls	**must**	**wear** school uniform.
What	**must**	the boys **wear**?
They	**must**	**wear** school uniform, too.
	Must	Barbara **wear** a pullover?
Yes, she	**must.**	

- Mit *must* drückt man eine Notwendigkeit oder Verpflichtung aus.
- Wie bei *can* bleibt auch das Hilfsverb *must* in allen Personen gleich.
- Es wird in Verbindung mit dem Infinitiv eines Verbs ohne *to* gebraucht: He must *go*.

17 Der unbestimmte Artikel   The indefinite article   Unit 3 Step 2

	a [ə]			**an** [ən]	
	a	**h**ouse		an	**e**mpty house
	a	**g**ood idea		an	**i**dea
This is	a	**d**ifficult exercise.	That's	an	**e**asy exercise.
They've got	a	**G**erman car.	We've got	an	**E**nglish car.
Is that	a	**n**ew blouse?	No, it's	an	**o**ld shirt!

- Immer wenn nach einem unbestimmten Artikel das Folgewort mit einem Vokal beginnt, verwendet man *an* [ən] statt *a* [ə].

 Der unbestimmte Artikel richtet sich nach der **Aussprache,** nicht nach der Schreibung des folgenden Worts. Vor einem **u**, das [juː] ausgesprochen wird, lautet er *a* (nicht *an*!): a unit, a uniform [ə ˈjuːnɪt, əˈjuːnɪfɔːm].

18 Der bestimmte Artikel   The definite article

	the [ðə]			**the** [ðɪ]	
	the	father		the	old man
	the	mother		the	English teacher
	the	house		the	empty house
	the	parents		the	answers
	the	cars		the	exercise books

- Im Englischen macht der bestimmte Artikel keinen Unterschied zwischen männlich, weiblich und sächlich oder zwischen Singular und Plural. Er wird immer *the* geschrieben: *the* heißt also *der, die* oder *das*.
- Die Aussprache von *the* richtet sich nach dem ersten Laut des folgenden Wortes: vor einem Konsonant wird er [ðə] ausgesprochen, vor einem Vokal [ðɪ].

 Vgl. §17. Ausschlaggebend ist die Aussprache, nicht die Schreibung des folgenden Wortes. So sagt man: the unit [ðə ˈjuːnɪt], the uniform [ðə ˈjuːnɪfɔːm].

Unit 3/Unit 4

§19 Der s-Genitiv, Plural   The s-genitive, plural   Unit 3 Step 3

Der s-Genitiv Plural zeigt an, zu welchen Personen jemand oder etwas gehört (siehe §6).

The friends are at the Klein**s'**	house.	Die Freunde sind im Haus der Kleins.	
Barbara is doing the boy**s'**	German homework.	Barbara macht die Deutsch-Hausaufgaben der Jungen.	
"Hey, Kate! That's my parent**s'**	bedroom.	"He, Kate! Das ist das Schlafzimmer meiner Eltern."	

Bei Wörtern, die schon ein Plural-s haben, wird beim Schreiben lediglich ein Apostroph (') hinter diesem Plural-s angehängt.

Unit 4

§20 Die Pluralform der Nomen   The plural of nouns   Unit 4 Step 1

- Der Plural wird gebildet, indem man ein *-s* an den Singular anhängt.
  Das *-s* wird unterschiedlich ausgesprochen. Beachte die Besonderheiten in Spalte 3 und 4!

[s]	[z]	[ɪz]	unregelmäßig
three bo**oks** two ca**ts** five du**cks** ten ma**ps**	five ba**gs** six car**ds** two do**gs** four bo**ys**	nine pa**ges** two pie**ces** eight blo**uses** seven bru**shes**	(a child) two child**ren** (one man) three m**en** (a woman) four wom**en**
• Nach den stimmlosen Lauten [p, t, k, f, θ] wird das *-s* stimmlos (scharf) ausgesprochen [s].	• Nach Vokalen und stimmhaften Konsonanten [b, d, g, n, m, v] wird das *-s* stimmhaft (weich) ausgesprochen [z].	• Nach den Zischlauten [s, z, dʒ, ʃ, tʃ] wird das *-s* [ɪz] ausgesprochen. Wenn kein stummes End-*e* vorhanden ist, muß ein *-e-* vor dem *-s* eingeschoben werden.	

1. *-y* nach einem Konsonanten wird im Plural zu *-ies*.
   bab*y* – bab*ies*
   famil*y* – famil*ies*

   Aber nach einem Vokal bleibt *-y* erhalten:
   bo*y* – bo*ys*
   to*y* – to*ys*

Unit 4

2. Beachte die unregelmäßige Aussprache bei: house [s] – houses [zɪz]

3.

a child	– two children [ˈtʃɪldrən]
one man	– three men [men]
a woman	– four women [ˈwɪmɪn]

- Einige Wörter haben einen unregelmäßigen Plural, ohne s.

| **women's** and **men's** **children's** | In this shop they've got shoes shoes, but they haven't got shoes. |

- Um den Genitiv dieser Pluralformen zu bilden, wird beim Sprechen ein [z] angehängt und beim Schreiben ein Apostroph (') und ein Genitiv-s.

21 'These/Those'

These/Those verwendet man, wenn man auf **mehrere** Gegenstände oder Personen zeigt (vgl. §13).

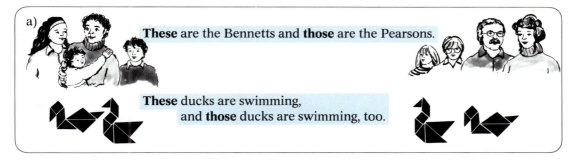

- Bei Gegenüberstellungen sagt man zuerst *these*, dann *those*.

- *These* kann auch auf Personen oder Dinge weisen, die **in der Nähe des Sprechers** sind, *those* auf Personen oder Dinge, die **weiter entfernt sind**.

Unit 4

§22 Die Kurzformen von 'have got/has got'   Unit 4 Step 2/3

	Singular		Plural
have got	I**'ve got** a blue pullover. You**'ve got** a blue shirt.	have got	We**'ve got** a new friend. You**'ve got** our address.
has got	He**'s got** a nice dog. She**'s got** a Tangram puzzle. It**'s got** seven pieces.		They**'ve got** a big house.

- Die Langformen *I have got, you have got, he has got* usw. werden – vor allem im gesprochenen Englisch – häufig zu *I've got, you've got, he's got* usw. verkürzt.

Halte auseinander: He's got a nice dog. = He has got (Er hat…) a nice dog.
He's a nice dog. = He is (Er ist…) a nice dog.

§23 Die Personalpronomen: Objektform   The personal pronouns: object form

Subjektform	Objektform			
I	"This is Mrs Morton. Can you drive	**me**	to the station?	…mich…
	Can you send	**me**	a taxi, please?"	…mir…
you	"Dad, here's a passenger for	**you.**		…dich…
	Let me give	**you**	the address."	…dir…
he	"Sorry, Ronny. I can't take	**him.**		…ihn…
	Send	**him**	another taxi."	…ihm…
she	"It's Mrs Morton, Dad. Can we take	**her**	to the station?"	…sie…
	"What about Mum? Give	**her**	the address."	…ihr…
it	"There's a horse! Can you see	**it,**	Timmy?	…es…
	Let's give	**it**	a name."	…ihm…
we	"Can you drive	**us**	into York, Dad?	…uns…
	Or can you give	**us**	a pound for the bus?"	…uns…
you	"Sorry, boys. I can't take	**you**	now.	…euch…
	Perhaps Mum can give	**you**	a pound.	…euch…
they	It's the boys, dear. Can you drive	**them**	into York?	…sie…
	No? O.K., then. Let's give	**them**	a pound for the bus."	…ihnen…

- Das Personalpronomen hat im Englischen nur eine Objektform.
Me kann z. B. *mir* oder *mich* heißen.

24 Der Imperativ (Befehlsform)
The imperative

Der Imperativ wird benutzt, um Anweisungen oder Befehle zu geben.

Go home	Geh Geht Gehen Sie	nach Hause!
Be quiet.	Sei Seid Seien Sie	ruhig!

- Der Imperativ hat die gleiche Form wie der Infinitiv (ohne *to*).
- Der Imperativ verändert sich nicht, ganz gleich, ob er an eine Person oder an mehrere Personen gerichtet ist.

Unit 5

25 Die Grundzahlen   The cardinal numbers   Unit 5 Step 1

1	one	11	eleven	21	twenty-one	40	forty
2	two	12	twelve	22	twenty-two	50	fifty
3	three	13	thirteen	23	twenty-three	60	sixty
4	four	14	fourteen	24	twenty-four	70	seventy
5	five	15	fifteen	25	twenty-five	80	eighty
6	six	16	sixteen	26	twenty-six	90	ninety
7	seven	17	seventeen	27	twenty-seven	100	a/one hundred
8	eight	18	eighteen	28	twenty-eight	200	two hundred
9	nine	19	nineteen	29	twenty-nine	350	three hundred and fifty
10	ten	20	twenty	30	thirty	999	nine hundred and ninety-nine

Achte auf die Rechtschreibung: four – fourteen – f**or**ty
five – fifteen – fifty
Achte auf die Aussprache: [faɪv] – [ˈfɪftiːn] – [ˈfɪftɪ]

Vor *hundred* muß immer der unbestimmte Artikel *a* oder ein Zahlwort (*one/two* usw.) stehen: *a hundred, one hundred, two hundred* usw.
Weitere Zahlen werden immer durch *and* angeschlossen: *a hundred and* ten (hundertzehn).

Unit 5

§ 26 Die Uhrzeit

Unit 5 Step 2

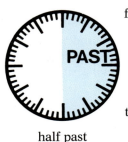

...o'clock
five (minutes) past...
ten (minutes) past...
(a) quarter past...
twenty (minutes) past...
twenty-five (minutes) past...
half past

...o'clock
five (minutes) to...
ten (minutes) to...
(a) quarter to...
twenty (minutes) to...
twenty-five (minutes) to...

1. Die ersten dreißig Minuten einer Stunde zählt man zur Stunde vorher dazu.
z. B.: 6.00: six o'clock
6.05: five past six
6.10: ten past six
6.15: (a) quarter past six
6.30: half past six

Beachte:
half past six
(deutsch: halb sieben)

2. Die restlichen neunundzwanzig Minuten zieht man von der folgenden Stunde ab.
z. B.: 6.45: (a) quarter to seven
6.50: ten to seven
6.55: five to seven
7.00: seven o'clock

§ 27 Das Präsens (Gegenwartsform)
The simple present

Unit 5 Steps 2/4

I	like	jumble sales.
You	like	picnics.
Kevin	**likes**	water-pistols.
Kate	**likes**	comics.
The dog	**likes**	biscuits.
We	play	hopscotch on Saturdays.
You	play	football together.
They	play	cards in the evening.

- Das Präsens hat in den meisten Personen die gleiche Form wie der Infinitiv (ohne *to*).

  In der 3. Person Singular *(he, she, it)* wird jedoch ein *-s* an das Verb angehängt (siehe § 28).

- Das *simple present* beschreibt Handlungen, die nicht jetzt gerade, sondern regelmäßig oder häufig geschehen *(every morning, every day, every week, often* usw.).
- Das *simple present* muß man auch verwenden, wenn man Handlungsfolgen beschreibt oder erzählt:
  First Wendy collects the children from school.
  Then she takes them home.
  After that she cleans her bus.

28 Die 3. Person Singular: Aussprache und Schreibung — Unit 5 Step 3

Wendy Webb	drives	a school bus.	
Every day she	sees	a lot of children.	[z]
In the evening she	cleans	her bus.	
She often	finds	things!	
Mr Pearson	starts	early.	
He	works	in the shop.	[s]
Sometimes he	writes	letters upstairs.	
The man often	teaches	his dog tricks.	[ɪz]

- Nach stimmhaften Konsonanten wie [d, n, v] und nach Vokalen wird das -s stimmhaft [z] ausgesprochen.
- Nach stimmlosen Konsonanten wie [p, t, k] wird es stimmlos [s] ausgesprochen.
- Nach Zischlauten wie [ʃ], [tʃ] wird -es angehängt und [ɪz] ausgesprochen.

 Vgl. § 20. Das -s/-es in der 3. Person Singular wird genauso ausgesprochen wie das -s/-es bei der Pluralbildung.

to carry:	He	carries	the box.
to fly:	It	flies	into the air.
to say:	She	says	'good morning'.
to go:	He	goes	to the park.
to do:	Bonzo	does	it again!

- Verben auf -y: Wenn ein Konsonant vorausgeht, wird die Endung -ies geschrieben.
- Das -y bleibt jedoch, wenn es nach einem Vokal steht.
- Go und do: an diese Verben wird -es angehängt.

 Beachte die Aussprache:
to go [gəʊ]   she goes [gəʊz]   **aber:** to do [duː]   she does [dʌz]
to play [pleɪ]   he plays [pleɪz]   **aber:** to say [seɪ]   he says [sez]

29 Die Wortstellung im bejahten Aussagesatz — Unit 5 Step 4

Subject	Verb	Object	
I	can play	football.	
Kevin	likes	old trains.	
She	has got	an orange.	
The friends	are making	their kite.	
We	have	lunch	at school.
They	must go	home	now.

- Die Wortstellung im englischen Aussagesatz lautet immer:
Subjekt – Verb – Objekt
S – V – O
Im Gegensatz zum Deutschen kann man diese Reihenfolge **nicht** umstellen.

 Nur nach der direkten Rede kann das Subjekt hinter dem Verb stehen, das ist genauso wie im Deutschen, z. B.: "What's the matter, Timmy?" **asks Ronny.**
"I want to go, too," **cries Timmy.**

Unit 5

§ 30 Die Stellung von Zeitangaben The position of expressions of time

Zeit	S	V	O	Ort	Zeit
Every morning	we	have	breakfast	in the kitchen.	
On Saturdays	Mr Wilson	takes	Bonzo	to the park.	
	Wendy	cleans	the bus		every afternoon.
	They	play	football	in the park	on Sundays.

- Zeitangaben können am Anfang oder am Ende des Satzes stehen, d. h. vor oder nach der S-V-O-Gruppe.
- Wenn man die Zeitangabe stärker betonen will, bringt man sie am Anfang.
- Stehen eine Orts- und eine Zeitangabe am Satzende, dann gilt: Ort vor Zeit. Man muß also erst den Ort nennen und dann die Zeitangabe machen.

§ 31 Die Stellung der Adverbien der Häufigkeit
The position of adverbs of frequency

S	Adv	V		
I	always	get up	at half past six.	Ich stehe immer um halb sieben auf.
We	usually	leave	at quarter past eight.	Wir gehen gewöhnlich um viertel nach acht.
Dad	sometimes	takes	us to school.	Vati fährt uns manchmal zur Schule.
They	often	read	comics in the afternoon.	Sie lesen oft Komikhefte am Nachmittag.

- Im Englischen steht das Adverb der Häufigkeit meist zwischen Subjekt und Verb, im Deutschen meist nach dem Verb.

Aber:

Don is	**always**	late.
He **can**	**never**	get to school on time.

- Das Adverb der Häufigkeit steht nach dem Verb *to be* und zwischen Hilfsverb und Infinitiv.

Unit 6

2 Gegenüberstellung: present progressive – simple present Unit 6 Step 1/3

a) **Die Verlaufsform des Präsens (present progressive)**

- Die Verlaufsform drückt aus, daß etwas **gerade jetzt** geschieht und **noch nicht vorbei** ist (siehe § 14).

b) **Das Präsens (simple present)** (siehe § 27)
   Mit dem *simple present* werden zwei verschiedene Arten von Handlungen beschrieben, nämlich:

1. **Gewohnheitsmäßige Handlungen**
   Mit dem *simple present* drückt man aus, daß etwas regelmäßig, oft, manchmal oder nie geschieht.

   Signalwörter: *every day, on (Saturdays), often, sometimes, never* usw.

Unit 6

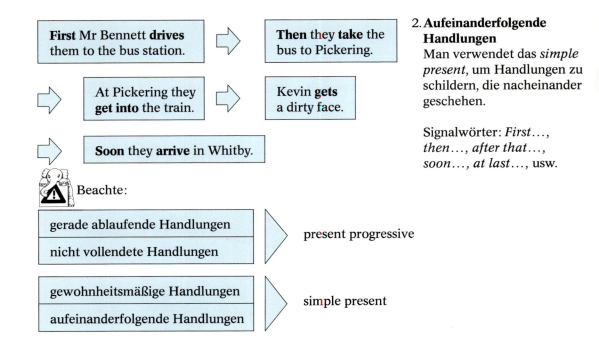

2. **Aufeinanderfolgende Handlungen**
Man verwendet das *simple present*, um Handlungen zu schildern, die nacheinander geschehen.

Signalwörter: *First…, then…, after that…, soon…, at last…,* usw.

§ 33 Mengenangaben mit 'of'
Expressions of quantity with 'of'

Unit 6 Step 2

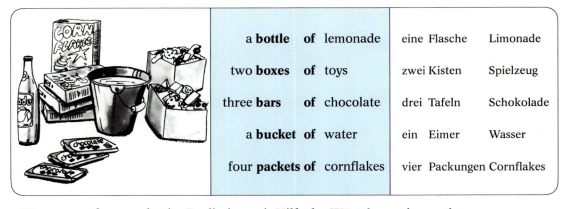

- Mengenangaben werden im Englischen mit Hilfe des Wörtchens *of* gemacht. Im Deutschen benötigt man ein entsprechendes Hilfswörtchen nicht.

Unit 7

4 Die Verneinung mit to do Unit 7 Steps 1/2/3

Aussagen mit einer Form von **to be** oder anderen Hilfsverben werden einfach durch das Einfügen von **not** verneint (vgl. §§ 3, 8, 12).

Beispiele: He **is not** from Germany.
They **aren't** watching TV.
I **can't** swim.
They **haven't** got a pet.

Verneinungen von Simple Present-Formen sind nur durch zusätzlichen Gebrauch **einer Form** von **to do** möglich.

a) Verneinung = do not + Infinitiv
     (don't)

I		like	milk.	Ich mag Milch.
I	**don't**	like	tea.	Ich mag keinen Tee.
You	**don't**	start	here.	Du fängst nicht hier an.
We	**don't**	live	in York.	Wir wohnen nicht in York.
You	**don't**	know	her.	Ihr kennt sie nicht.
They	**don't**	come	from York.	Sie kommen nicht aus York.

b) 3. Person (he, she, it)
Bejahende Aussage: She sells cars.
Verneinung: But he doesn't sell cars.

Verneinung 3. Person = does not + Infinitiv
       (doesn't)

He	**doesn't**	sell	cars.	Er verkauft keine Autos.
She	**doesn't**	drive	a school bus.	Sie fährt keinen Schulbus.
It	**doesn't**	rain	every day.	Es regnet nicht jeden Tag.
The train	**doesn't**	stop	at Grosmont.	Der Zug hält nicht in Grosmont.
Ronny	**doesn't**	like	milk.	Ronny mag keine Milch.

§35 Entscheidungsfragen mit 'do/does'
Yes/no questions with 'do/does'

Unit 7 Step 2

Entscheidungsfragen sind Fragen, die man mit „ja" oder „nein" beantworten muß. Solche Fragen können mit Formen von *to be* oder anderen Hilfsverben wie *can, must, have/has* beginnen (§ 4, § 9, § 12, § 16):

Can you swim? – Yes, I can.
Must you go? – Yes, we must.
Are you ill? – No, I'm not.

Bei der Simple Present-Form aber beginnt die Frage mit *do/does*.

Entscheidungsfrage				Kurzantwort	
Do	I	look	nice?	Yes,	you do.
Do	you	know	Mr Brown?	No,	I don't.
Does	he	live	in Selby Road?	Yes,	he does.
Does	she	like	oranges?	Yes,	she does.
Does	it	rain	every Saturday?	No,	it doesn't.
Do	we	start	here?	Yes,	you do.
Do	you	like	this game?	Yes,	we do.
Do	they	sell	felt pens?	No,	they don't.

1. Wird die Entscheidungsfrage mit *do/does* formuliert, erscheint eine Form von *do* auch in der Kurzantwort.

Hv	S	V	O
	You	know	Mr Brown.
Do	you	know	Mr White?
	He	sell**s**	cars.
Does	he	sell	vans?

2. Bei Fragen mit *do/does* bleibt das englische Satzmuster S – V – O erhalten.

3. Das Vollverb steht immer im Infinitiv (ohne *to*).
4. Bei *he, she, it* bleibt das *s*, allerdings nicht bei der Grundform des Verbs, sondern bei dem *does*.

§36 Fragen mit Fragewörtern und 'do/does'
Questions with question words and 'do/does'

Unit 7 Step 3

Fragen mit Fragewörtern wie *when, what, where* usw. werden ähnlich gebildet wie Entscheidungsfragen (vgl. §35). Auf das Fragewort kann eine Form von *to be* oder ein anderes Hilfsverb folgen:

When **are** you coming?
What **can** you see?

Bei der Simple Present-Form aber beginnt die Frage mit dem Fragewort + *do/does*.

	Hv	S	V	O	
When	do	you	get	home from school?	At half past four.
What	do	you	do	then?	We sometimes go to Barbara's house.
Where	does	she	live?		She lives next door.
Why	do	you	go	to her house?	Because she can speak German.
How	does	that	help	you?	We do our German homework together!

57 Der verneinte Imperativ (verneinte Befehlsform)   Unit 7 Step 3
The negative imperative

Wenn man jemanden ermahnen oder überreden oder ihm sogar befehlen möchte, etwas nicht zu tun, verwendet man den verneinten Imperativ (Befehlsform).

Don't	be	late, Barbara!	Komm nicht zu spät, Barbara!
Don't	sell	your car, Mr Bennett!	Verkaufen Sie Ihr Auto nicht, Herr Bennett!
Don't	play	football in the attic!	Spielt auf dem Dachboden nicht Fußball!

- Der verneinte Imperativ wird immer mit don't + **Infinitiv** gebildet, ganz gleich, ob eine Person oder mehrere Personen angesprochen sind.

Register des Grammatikanhangs

	Seite
Adverbien der Häufigkeit (§ 31)	134
Artikel	
bestimmter Artikel (§ 18)	127
unbestimmter Artikel (§ 17)	127
to be	
Kurz- und Langformen (§ 1)	120
Fragen und Kurzantworten (§ 4)	121
Verneinung (§ 3)	121
bestimmter Artikel (§ 18)	127
can (§ 12)	124
do/does	
Entscheidungsfragen (§ 35)	138
Fragen mit Fragewörtern (§ 36)	138
Verneinung (§ 34)	137
Entscheidungsfragen mit *do/does* (§ 35)	138
Fragen mit Fragewörtern + *do/does* (§ 36)	138
Fragen und Kurzantworten	
mit *to be* (§ 4)	121
mit *do/does* (§ 35)	138
mit *have got/has got* (§ 9)	123
mit *can* (§ 12)	124
Fragewörter *where, who, what,* (§ 10)	123
***s*-Genitiv**	
Plural (§ 19/20.3)	128/129
Singular (§ 6)	122
Grundzahlen (§ 25)	131
have got/has got (§ 7)	122
Verneinung (§ 8)	123
Fragen und Kurzantworten (§ 9)	123
Kurzformen (§ 22)	130
Hilfsverben	
can (§ 12)	124
must (§ 16)	127
Imperativ (§ 24)	131
der verneinte Imperativ (§ 37)	139
Kurzformen	
to be (§ 1)	120
have got/has got (§ 22)	130

	Seite
Zusammenstellung (§ 11)	124
Mengenangaben mit *of* (§ 33)	136
must (§ 16)	127
Personalpronomen	
Subjektform (§ 2)	120
Objektform (§ 23)	130
Plural der Nomen (§ 20)	128
Possessivpronomen (§ 5)	122
Präsens	
present progressive (§ 14/15)	126
simple present (§ 27/28)	132/133
3. Person Singular (§ 28)	133
Gegenüberstellung: *present progressive – simple present* (§ 32)	135
-*s* in der 3. Person Singular (§ 28)	133
***s*-Genitiv**	
Plural (§ 19/20.3)	128/129
Singular (§ 6)	122
these/those (§ 21)	129
this/that (§ 13)	125
Uhrzeit (§ 26)	132
unbestimmter Artikel (§ 17)	127
Verlaufsform des Präsens (§ 14/15)	126
Verneinung	
to be (§ 3)	121
mit *don't/doesn't* (§ 34)	137
have got/has got (§ 8)	123
verneinter Imperativ (§ 37)	139
where, who, what, (§ 10)	123
Wortstellung	
von Adverbien der Häufigkeit (§ 31)	134
im bejahten Aussagesatz (§ 29)	133
bei Fragen (§ 35, § 36)	138
von Zeitangaben (§ 30)	134
Zahlen	
Grundzahlen (§ 25)	131

Vocabulary

Lautzeichen (Phonetic Symbols)

Vokale (Vowels)

[ɑ:] father, cards; langes *a*, weiter hinten gesprochen als in *Vater*

[ʌ] mother, does, brush; kurzes *a*, etwa wie in *Mann*

[e] pen, head; etwa wie das *e* in *nett*

[ə] a bar of chocolate, sister; kurzer, unbetonter Laut, wie der Endlaut in *bitte*

[ɜ:] girl, her, word; etwa ein verlängertes [ə]. Dieser Laut wird weiter hinten gesprochen als das deutsche *ö* (Lippen nicht vorstülpen!)

[æ] flat, van; kurzes, ganz offenes *ä*, offener als in *Männer*

[ɪ] it, bucket; kurzes *i* wie in *Lippe*, doch weniger spitz, etwas zum [ə] hin

[i:] teacher, she, piece; langes *i* wie in *tief*

[ɒ] shop, what; kurzes, offenes *o*

[ɔ:] or, door, four; langes, offenes *o* (Lippen leicht vorstülpen!)

[ʊ] pullover, look; kurzes *u* wie in *Schutt*

[u:] you, too, blue; langes *u*, etwa wie in *du* (Lippen kaum vorstülpen!)

Doppellaute (Diphthongs)

[aɪ] nine, by, right; wie *ai* in *Mai, Kaiser*

[aʊ] now, house; helles *a* mit nachklingendem *u*, etwa wie in *Zauber*

[eə] there, chair; kurzes, offenes *ä* mit nachklingendem [ə], etwa wie in *Bär*

[eɪ] name, they, eight; englisches [e] mit nachklingendem [ɪ]

[ɪə] here, idea; etwa wie in *mir*

[ɔɪ] boy; kurzes offenes *o* mit nachklingendem [ɪ], ähnlich wie in *Freude*

[əʊ] hello, road; [ə] mit nachklingendem [ʊ]

[ʊə] moors, tourist; [ʊ] mit nachklingendem [ə]

Konsonanten (Consonants)

[j] yes, new; wie das deutsche *j*

[l] listen, blue; am Wortanfang und vor Vokalen etwa wie das deutsche *l* school, shelf; am Wortende und vor Konsonanten wie das *l* der Rheinländer, z. B. in *Köln*

[ŋ] morning, long; wie der -*ng*-Laut in *singen* (kein [g] sprechen!)

[ŋg] English; wie [ŋ] jedoch mit nachfolgendem gesprochenem [g]

[r] red, brush; Gaumen-*r*, Zungenspitze gegen Gaumen anheben und leicht zurückbiegen; der austretende Luftstrom erzeugt [r]

[s] sister, this; stimmloses, d. h. hartes *s* wie in *Laus*

[z] is, dogs; stimmhaftes, d. h. weiches *s* wie in *summen*

[ʒ] garage; stimmhaftes *sch* wie in *Gelee*

[dʒ] jeans, German; [ʒ] mit vorausklingendem [d]

[ʃ] she, station; stimmloses *sch* wie in *Tisch*

[tʃ] teacher, child; [ʃ] mit vorausklingendem [t]

[st/sp] story, sport; wird [st] und [sp] gesprochen, nicht [ʃt] und [ʃp]

[ð] the, mother; stimmhafter Lispellaut (Zunge zwischen den Zähnen!)

[θ] thanks, nothing; stimmloser Lispellaut (Zunge zwischen den Zähnen!)

[v] van, of; wie *w* in *Winter*

[w] week, which, one; vom [ʊ] ausgehen und zum folgenden Laut hinübergleiten

ˈ = Hauptbetonung
ˌ = Nebenbetonung
(Die Betonungsstriche stehen immer **vor** der betonten Silbe.)

‿ = besonders enge Bindung zweier Worte aneinander

First Scenes

° Die mit ° gekennzeichneten Wörter gehören zum rezeptiven Wortschatz. Zur Differenzierung kann der rezeptive Wortschatz auch produktiv verlangt werden.
⟨ ⟩ Stücke, deren Überschriften, und Übungen, deren Ziffern in Winkelklammern stehen, sind fakultativ.
Die Texte und Übungen des Additums können auch einzeln durchgenommen werden. Im Vokabular des Additums werden alle Wörter aufgeführt, die zum Zeitpunkt der vorgeschlagenen Durchnahme des Additums im Fundamentum noch unbekannt sind.

First Scenes

first °scenes	[fɜːst ˈsiːnz]	erste Szenen
York	[jɔːk]	York *(Stadt im Nordosten Englands)*

1 Good morning

	Good morning.	[gʊd ˈmɔːnɪŋ]	Guten Morgen!
a)	teacher	[ˈtiːtʃə]	Lehrer, Lehrerin
	I'm (= I am)	[aɪm]	ich bin
	your	[jɔː]	dein(e), euer(e), Ihr(e)
	My name is...	[maɪ ˈneɪm‿ɪz]	Ich heiße...
	my		mein
	name		Name
	is		ist
	Mrs Griffin	[ˌmɪsɪz ˈgrɪfɪn]	Frau Griffin
b)	hello	[heˈləʊ]	hallo, guten Tag
	new	[njuː]	neu
	boy	[bɔɪ]	Junge
	What is your name?	[ˌwɒt‿ɪz jɔː ˈneɪm]	Wie heißt du? Wie heißen Sie?
	what		was

Exercises

	exercise	[ˈeksəsaɪz]	Übung
	°dialogues	[ˈdaɪəlɒgz]	°Dialoge
4	Over to you.	[ˌəʊvə tə ˈjuː]	Du bist/Ihr seid/Sie sind dran.

2 Kevin

a)	not	[nɒt]	nicht
	Oh, sorry.	[əʊ ˈsɒrɪ]	Oh, Entschuldigung! Tut mir leid.
b)	Are you new?	[ɑː juː ˈnjuː]	Bist du/Seid Ihr/Sind Sie neu?
	you		du, Ihr, Sie
	yes	[jes]	ja
	You are in °1 B.	[jɔːr‿ɪn wʌn ˈbiː]	Du bist in Klasse °1 B.
	Thank you.	[ˈθæŋk‿juː]	Danke schön.

Exercises

2	no	[nəʊ]	nein
	Look, listen and say.	[ˈlʊk ˈlɪsn nˈseɪ]	Schau(t) hin, hör(t) zu und sprich (sprecht) nach!
	to look		schauen, gucken
	to listen		zuhören
	to say		sagen
	and	[ənd]	und

First Scenes

3 Sorry, no idea

	no idea	[ˈnəʊ_aɪˈdɪə]	keine Ahnung
	no		kein(e)
	idea		Idee, Vorstellung, Ahnung
a)	**Look at that boy.**	[ˈlʊk_ət ðæt ˈbɔɪ]	Sieh dir/Seht euch/Sehen Sie sich den Jungen an!
	to look at		anschauen
	that		der/die/das da
	he is	[hi: ɪz]	er ist
	girl	[gɜ:l]	Mädchen
	°1 A	[wʌn ˈeɪ]	°Klasse 1 A
	his name	[hɪz]	sein Name
b)	**Is she new?**	[ˈɪz ʃi:ˈnju:]	Ist sie neu?
	the	[ðə]	der/die/das
	English	[ˈɪŋglɪʃ]	englisch
	her name	[hɜ: ˈneɪm]	ihr Name

4 The new boy

a)	boys and girls	[ˈbɔɪz_n ˈgɜ:lz]	Jungen und Mädchen
b)	where	[weə]	wo
	register	[ˈredʒɪstə]	Klassenbuch
	It's here.	[ɪts ˈhɪə]	Es ist hier.
	it's (= it is)		es ist
	She's ill.	[ʃi:z_ˈɪl]	Sie ist krank.
	she's (= she is)		sie ist
c)	**He's late.**	[hi:z ˈleɪt]	Er kommt zu spät.
	you're (= you are)	[jɔ:]	du bist/Sie sind/ihr seid
	I'm sorry	[aɪm ˈsɒrɪ]	Es tut mir leid.
d)	**What is your name, please?**	[ˌwɒt_ɪz jɔ: ˈneɪm ˌpli:z]	Wie heißt du bitte?
	Where are you from?	[ˈweər_ə jʊ ˈfrɒm]	Wo kommst du her?
	I'm from Leeds.	[ˌaɪm frəm ˈli:dz]	Ich komme/bin aus Leeds.
	from		von, aus
	Leeds		*Stadt im Norden Englands*

Exercises

1	**Questions and answers**	[ˈkwestʃənz_n_ˈɑ:nsəz]	Fragen und Antworten
	question		Frage
	answer		Antwort
2	**Find the right words.**	[ˈfaɪnd ðe raɪt ˈwɜ:dz]	Finde(t) die richtigen Wörter!
	to find		finden
	right		richtig
	word		Wort
	I am	[aɪ_ˈæm]	ich bin
4	**Make questions.**	[ˈmeɪk ˈkwestʃənz]	Bilde(t) Fragen.
	to make		machen, bilden
	°example	[ɪgˈzɑ:mpl]	°Beispiel

First Scenes

5 Selby Road

	road	[rəʊd]	Straße
a)	house	[haʊs]	Haus
	It's a flat, not a house.	[ə 'flæt 'nɒt ə 'haʊs]	Es ist eine Wohnung, kein Haus.
	a	[ə]	ein, eine
	we're (= we are)	[wɪə]	wir sind
	too	[tu:]	auch
	good	[gʊd]	gut, prima
b)	Look, **that is** ...	['lʊk 'ðæt ɪz]	Schau(t) mal, das ist ...
	our	[aʊə]	unser(e)
	shop	[ʃɒp]	Laden
	father	['fɑːðə]	Vater
	mother	['mʌðə]	Mutter
	van	[væn]	Lieferwagen
	on the van	[ɒn]	auf dem Lieferwagen
	sister	['sɪstə]	Schwester
	terrible	['terəbl]	fürchterlich, schrecklich, *hier:* unmöglich
	brother	['brʌðə]	Bruder

Exercises

1	**Ask** your **friends**.	['ɑːsk jɔː 'frendz]	Frage deine Freunde!
	to ask		fragen
	friend		Freund, Freundin
2	**or**	[ɔː]	oder
	Mr Pearson	['mɪstə]	Herr Pearson
5	example**s**	[ɪgˈzɑːmplz]	Beispiele

Revision

---

you = du, ihr, Sie

You're late, Ben.	**Du** kommst zu spät, Ben.
You're late, Ben and Penny.	**Ihr** kommt zu spät, Ben und Penny.
You're late, Mrs Griffin.	**Sie** kommen zu spät, Frau Griffin.

your = dein(e), euer(e), Ihr(e)

Is that **your** friend, Helen?	Ist das **deine** Freundin/**dein** Freund, Helen?
Is that **your** friend, Helen and Kevin?	Ist das **eure** Freundin/**euer** Freund, Helen und Kevin?
Is that **your** flat, Mrs Pearson?	Ist das **Ihre** Wohnung, Frau Pearson?
Is that **your** van, Mrs Pearson?	Ist das **Ihr** Lieferwagen, Frau Pearson?

Look at that shop, Jenny.	**Sieh dir** den Laden da an, Jenny!
Look at that shop, Jenny and Ben.	**Seht euch** den Laden da an, Jenny und Ben!
Look at that shop, Mrs Bennett.	**Sehen Sie sich** den Laden da an, Frau Bennett!

6 The Pearsons

a) She isn't in the flat. [ʃi: 'ɪznt] Sie ist nicht in der Wohnung.
   she isn't (= she is not) sie ist nicht
   Is she in the van? Ist sie im Lieferwagen?
   No, she isn't. ['nəʊ ʃi: 'ɪznt] Nein, (da ist sie nicht).
   Mum [mʌm] Mutti, Mama
b) man [mæn] Mann
   they're (= they are) [ðeə] sie sind
   their name [ðeə 'neɪm] ihr Name
c) woman ['wʊmən] Frau
   Are they from York? [ˌɑ: ðeɪ frəm 'jɔ:k] Sind sie aus York?
   No, they aren't. [ðeɪ 'ɑ:nt] Nein.
   they aren't (= they are) not sie sind nicht

Exercises

2 Answer the questions. [ˌɑ:nsə ðə 'kwestʃənz] Beantworte(t) die Fragen.
   to answer beantworten

7 The new shop

a) dirty ['dɜ:tɪ] schmutzig
   floor [flɔ:] Fußboden
   window ['wɪndəʊ] Fenster
   door [dɔ:] Tür
   cupboard ['kʌbəd] Schrank
   chair [tʃeə] Stuhl
   clean [kli:n] sauber
b) She has got a box. [ʃi: həz gɒt‿ə 'bɒks] Sie hat einen Karton.
   box Karton, Kiste, Schachtel
   under her arm ['ʌndə hər‿'ɑ:m] unter dem Arm
   sponge [spʌndʒ] Schwamm
   He hasn't got a box. [hi:'hæznt gɒt] Er hat keinen Karton.
   but [bʌt] aber
   bucket ['bʌkɪt] Eimer
   brush [brʌʃ] Besen, Bürste, Schrubber
   water ['wɔ:tə] Wasser
c) now [naʊ] jetzt
   behind the door [bɪ'haɪnd] hinter der Tür
   in front of the shop [ɪn 'frʌnt‿əv] vor dem Geschäft
   water-pistol ['wɔ:tə ˌpɪstl] Wasserpistole
   He hasn't got a water-pistol. – Yes, he has. Er hat keine Wasserpistole. – Doch!
   Come on. [ˌkʌm‿'ɒn] Los! Gehen wir! Komm schon!
   °Oh dear! [ˌəʊ 'dɪə] °Oje! Ach du meine Güte!

Exercises

2 What has Mrs Pearson got? Was hat Frau Pearson?
3 Has Mr Pearson got a bucket? – Yes, he has. ['jes hi: 'hæz] Hat Herr Pearson einen Eimer? – Ja.
   Has Mrs Pearson got a bucket? – No, she hasn't. ['nəʊ ʃi: 'hæznt] Hat Frau Pearson einen Eimer? – Nein.
8 taxi ['tæksɪ] Taxi

First Scenes

8 Ronny

a)	**I have got** a new friend.	[aɪ hæv ˈgɒt]	Ich habe einen neuen Freund.
	parents	[ˈpeərənts]	Eltern
b)	**Who** is that?	[ˌhuː ɪz ˈðæt]	Wer ist das?
	°**baby brother**	[ˈbeɪbɪ ˈbrʌðə]	°kleiner Bruder
	°**baby**		°Baby
	great	[greɪt]	prima, großartig
c)	**next door**	[neks ˈdɔː]	nebenan
	empty	[ˈemptɪ]	leer
	There is a taxi in front of Ronny's house.	[ˈðeər ɪz ə ˈtæksɪ]	Da steht ein Taxi vor Ronnys Haus.
	two	[tuː]	zwei
	taxi driver	[ˈtæksɪ ˌdraɪvə]	Taxifahrer(in)

Exercises

1	**Have the Bennetts got** a shop? – **No, they haven't.**		Haben die Bennetts einen Laden? – Nein.
	cat	[kæt]	Katze
5	**Is there** a bucket on the floor? – **No, there isn't.**		Steht da ein Eimer auf dem Boden? – Nein.

9 Timmy

a)	**in the morning**	[ɪn ðə ˈmɔːnɪŋ]	morgens, vormittags
	His mother is **out** in the taxi.	[hɪz ˈmʌðər ɪz ˌaʊt]	Seine Mutter ist mit dem Taxi unterwegs.
	out		nicht zu Hause
	at school	[ət ˈskuːl]	in der Schule
	at home	[ət ˈhəʊm]	zu Hause
	in the afternoon	[ɪn ðɪ ˌɑːftəˈnuːn]	nachmittags
	in the evening	[ɪn ðɪ ˈiːvnɪŋ]	abends
	°**so...**	[səʊ]	°also, deshalb
	sometimes	[ˈsʌmtaɪmz]	manchmal
	at night	[ət ˈnaɪt]	nachts
	Well, ...	[wel]	Also, ...
	all	[ɔːl]	alle
	in bed	[bed]	im Bett
b)	**telephone**	[ˈteləfəʊn]	Telefon
	toy	[tɔɪ]	Spielzeug

Exercises

2	°**teddy**	[ˈtedɪ]	°Teddy(bär)
	dog	[dɒg]	Hund
	Now you go on.	[naʊ ˈjuː gəʊ ˌɒn]	Mach du/Macht ihr jetzt weiter.
	to go on		weitermachen, fortfahren
⟨4⟩	Let's sing a song.	[lets sɪŋ ə ˈsɒŋ]	Laß(t) uns ein Lied singen.

Unit 1

| °unit | [ˈjuːnɪt] | °Einheit, *hier:* Lektion |

Step 1 Barbara

	step	[step]	Stufe, Schritt, Phase
a)	today	[təˈdeɪ]	heute
	there's (= there is)	[ðeəz]	dort ist, da ist
	where's (= where is)	[weəz]	wo ist
	car	[kɑː]	Auto
	'GB'	[dʒiː ˈbiː]	GB-Schild
	'D'	[diː]	D-Schild
	That's for Denmark.	[ˈðæts fə ˈdenmɑːk]	Das steht für Dänemark.
	that's (= that is)		das ist
	Germany	[ˈdʒɜːmənɪ]	Deutschland
b)	at the window	[æt ðə ˈwɪndəʊ]	am Fenster
	what's (= what is)		was ist
	German	[ˈdʒɜːmən]	deutsch
	My father is German.		Mein Vater ist Deutscher.

Exercises

1	who's (= who is)		wer ist
2	long	[lɒŋ]	lang
	°forms	[fɔːmz]	°Formen
	short	[ʃɔːt]	kurz
	be careful		Sei vorsichtig! Paß auf!
G	here's (= here is)		hier ist

Step 2 Can you speak English?

	Can you speak English?	[ˈkæn juː ˌspiːk]	Kannst du Englisch (sprechen)?
	can		können
	to speak		sprechen
a)	with	[wɪð]	mit
	Cologne	[kəˈləʊn]	Köln
	in English	[ɪn ˈɪŋglɪʃ]	auf englisch
	You're °lucky.	[ˈlʌkɪ]	°Du hast Glück! Du hast es gut!
b)	to write	[raɪt]	schreiben
	She can read German books.	[ʃiː kən riːd ˈdʒɜːmən bʊks]	Sie kann deutsche Bücher lesen.
	to read		lesen
	book		Buch

Exercises

1	What about Ronny?	[ˈwɒt_əˈbaʊt]	Was ist mit Ronny? Wie steht's mit Ronny?
	He can't speak German.	[hiː ˈkɑːnt]	Er kann kein Deutsch (sprechen).
3	newspaper	[ˈnjuːzpeɪpə]	Zeitung
	magazine	[ˌmægəˈziːn]	Zeitschrift
	comic	[ˈkɒmɪk]	Comic

Unit 1/Unit 2

°family	['fæməli]	°Familie
The mother is °**Danish**.	['deɪnɪʃ]	Die Mutter ist °Dänin.
That's **wrong**.	[rɒŋ]	Das stimmt nicht! Das ist falsch!
wrong		falsch

Revision

> **kein, keine**
>
> **No** idea.   **Keine** Ahnung.
> It's a flat, **not a** house.   Es ist eine Wohnung, **kein** Haus.
> Ben **hasn't got a** water-pistol.   Ben **hat keine** Wasserpistole.
> Kate **can't** speak German.   Kate **kann kein** Deutsch.

Step 3   Let's test Barbara's English

	let's (= let us)	[lets]	laß(t) uns
	°to test	[test]	°prüfen, abfragen
a)	**to play**	[pleɪ]	spielen
	O.K., Barbara?	[ˌəʊ'keɪ]	In Ordnung, Barbara?
	first	[fɜːst]	zuerst
	then	[ðen]	dann
	I'm next.	[aɪm 'nekst]	Ich bin der nächste.
b)	What's **this** in English?	[wɒts 'ðɪs ɪn ‿'ɪŋglɪʃ]	Wie heißt dies auf englisch?
	pen	[pen]	Füller, Füllfederhalter
	pencil	['pensl]	Bleistift
	biro	['baɪrəʊ]	Kugelschreiber
	rubber	['rʌbə]	Radiergummi
	ruler	['ruːlə]	Lineal
	felt pen	['felt pen]	Filzstift
	What's the word **for** this?	['wɒts ðə wɜːd fɔː 'ðɪs]	Wie heißt das Wort hierfür?
c)	It has got pencils **in it**.	[ɪt həz gɒt 'penslz ɪn‿ɪt]	Es sind Bleistifte darin.
	pencil case	['penslkeɪs]	Federmappe
	map	[mæp]	Karte
	This is a **school-bag**.	[ðɪs‿ɪz ə 'skuːl bæg]	Dies (hier) ist eine Schultasche.
	That's a map **over there**.	[ðæts‿ə 'mæp ˌəʊvə 'ðeə]	Das ist eine Landkarte dort drüben.

Exercises

2 °**vocabulary**	[vəʊ'kæbjʊləri]	°Wortschatz

⟨**Authentic Britain: At the newsagent's**⟩

authentic	[ɔː'θentɪk]	echt, authentisch
Britain	['brɪtn]	(Groß-)Britannien
at the newsagent's	[æt ðə 'njuːzeɪdʒənts]	beim Zeitungshändler

Unit 2

⟨**Photo page: Work and play**⟩

photo page	['fəʊtəʊpeɪdʒ]	Fotoseite

148   *one hundred and forty-eight*

Unit 2

work and play ['wɜːk_n 'pleɪ] Arbeit und Spiel

Step 1 One, two, three...

1 **How old** are you? [haʊ 'əʊld_ə juː] Wie alt bist du?
  how wie
  old alt
  eleven [ɪ'levn] elf
  ten [ten] zehn
  °**nearly** ['nɪəlɪ] °beinahe, fast
  twelve [twelv] zwölf
  sixteen [ˌsɪks'tiːn] sechzehn
  She's **still** in Germany [stɪl] Sie ist noch bei meinem Vater in
    with my father. [wɪð]   Deutschland.
    °**still** °noch
    with mit, bei

Exercises

2 **telephone numbers** ['teləfəʊn 'nʌmbəz] Telefonnummern
  °**police** [pə'liːs] °Polizei
  °**oh** [əʊ] °null
  °**double oh** ['dʌbl_əʊ] °null null
4 £2 (= two pounds) [ˌtuː 'paʊndz] zwei Pfund *(englische Währung)*
  How many have they got? ['haʊ ˌmenɪ] Wie viele haben sie?
5 How many **are there**? ['haʊ ˌmenɪ 'ɑː ðeə] Wie viele sind es?
  table ['teɪbl] Tisch
6 **game** [geɪm] Spiel

Revision

> there is, there are
>
> **There is** a van in front of the school. **Da steht** ein Lieferwagen vor der Schule.
> **There is** a girl at the window. Ein Mädchen **steht** am Fenster.
> **There are** five books on the table. **Es sind** fünf Bücher auf dem Tisch.
> **There are** two cupboards in the shop. **Es stehen** zwei Schränke in dem Laden.

Step 2 Can I help?

  to help [help] helfen
a) Can you **drive me to** Leeds? [kən juː 'draɪv mɪ tʊ Können Sie mich nach Leeds fahren?
    'liːdz]
  to drive fahren
  me mich
  to Leeds nach Leeds
b) Can you **run** to the shop [rʌn] Kannst du zum Laden laufen und eine
  for a newspaper? [fər_ə]   Zeitung holen?
c) **you** [juː] dir, euch, Ihnen
  to clean [kliːn] reinigen, saubermachen, putzen
  to do [duː] machen, tun
  to carry ['kærɪ] tragen

Unit 2

d)	to go for a walk	[ˌgəʊ fər_ə 'wɔːk]	spazierengehen
	walk		Spaziergang
	to wear	[weə]	tragen
	pullover	['pʊlˌəʊvə]	Pullover, Pulli

Exercises

1	sentences	['sentənsɪz]	Sätze

Step 3 Saturday morning

	Saturday	['sætədeɪ]	Samstag, Sonnabend
a)	10 o'clock	[ten_ə'klɒk]	10 Uhr
	on Saturday morning		am Samstag vormittag
	Mr Pearson **is cleaning** the van.	['kliːnɪŋ]	Mr Pearson putzt (gerade) den Lieferwagen.
	to play °hopscotch	['hɒpskɒtʃ]	°Huckekasten/Himmel-und-Hölle-spielen
	to watch	[wɒtʃ]	zuschauen
	to sit	[sɪt]	sitzen
	wall	[wɔːl]	Mauer, Wand
	The sun is shining.	[ðə ˌsʌn_ɪz 'ʃaɪnɪŋ]	Die Sonne scheint
	sun		Sonne
	to shine		scheinen
b)	It **is raining**.	[ɪt_ɪz 'reɪnɪŋ]	Es regnet.
	to rain		regnen
	into the shop	['ɪntʊ]	in den Laden (hinein)
	to run	[rʌn]	rennen, laufen
	funny	['fʌnɪ]	witzig

Exercises

3	picture**s**	['pɪktʃəz]	Bilder
	on page 40	[peɪdʒ 'fɔːtɪ]	auf Seite 40

Step 4 12 o'clock

	room	[ruːm]	Zimmer
	What are you doing?	['wɒt_ə juː 'dʊɪŋ]	Was tust du/tut ihr?
	to play **cards**	[kɑːdz]	Karten spielen
	to come	[kʌm]	kommen
	bathroom	['bɑːθrʊm]	Badezimmer
	to wait	[weɪt]	warten
	°potty	['pɒtɪ]	°Töpfchen

Exercises

2	to watch **TV**	[ˌtiː'viː]	fernsehen
5	**brown**	[braʊn]	braun
G	**We are waiting for** the girls.	[ˌwiːə 'weɪtɪŋ fə ðə 'gɜːlz]	Wir warten auf die Mädchen.
⟨6⟩	my Bonnie	[maɪ 'bɒnɪ]	meine Geliebte, mein Schatz
	...is over the ocean	['əʊʃn]	...ist über den Ozean (gefahren)
	...is over the sea	[siː]	...ist über das Meer (gefahren)
	to bring back	[ˌbrɪŋ 'bæk]	zurückbringen

Unit 3

⟨**Photo page: British school children**⟩

British school children	['brɪtɪʃ 'sku:l ˌtʃɪldrən]	britische Schulkinder
school colours	['sku:l 'kʌləz]	Farben von Schuluniform, -abzeichen usw.
red	[red]	rot
white	[waɪt]	weiß
comprehensive school	[ˌkɒmprɪ'hensɪv ˌsku:l]	Gesamtschule

Step 1 School uniform

school °uniform	['sku:l 'ju:nɪfɔ:m]	°Schuluniform
at a lot of schools	[ət ə 'lɒt əv 'sku:lz]	in vielen Schulen
a lot of		viel(e)
Britain	['brɪtn]	(Groß-)Britannien
they must (wear ...)	[mʌst]	sie müssen (... tragen)
school colours	['sku:l 'kʌləz]	Farben von Schuluniform, -abzeichen usw.
blue	[blu:]	blau
grey	[greɪ]	grau
skirt	[skɜ:t]	Rock
white	[waɪt]	weiß
blouse	[blaʊz]	Bluse
black	[blæk]	schwarz
shoe	[ʃu:]	Schuh
°tights	[taɪts]	°Strumpfhose
sock	[sɒk]	Socke, Kniestrumpf
trousers	['traʊzəz]	Hose
shirt	[ʃɜ:t]	Hemd
°blazer	['bleɪzə]	°Blazer
jeans	[dʒi:nz]	Jeans
red	[red]	rot
yellow	['jeləʊ]	gelb
green	[gri:n]	grün

Exercises

1	°comprehension	[ˌkɒmprɪ'henʃn]	(Fragen zum) °Textverständnis
2	What colour is it?	[wɒt 'kʌlər ɪz ɪt]	Welche Farbe hat er/sie/es?
4	the °missing words	['mɪsɪŋ]	°die fehlenden Wörter

Step 2 Homework

homework	['həʊmwɜ:k]	Hausaufgaben
a) °Comprehensive School	[ˌkɒmprɪ'hensɪv]	°Gesamtschule
bedroom	['bedrʊm]	Schlafzimmer
They are doing their homework together.	[tə'geðə]	Sie machen ihre Hausaufgaben zusammen.
b) °textbook	['tekstbʊk]	°Schulbuch

Unit 3

an English book	[æn]	ein Englischbuch
thanks	[θæŋks]	danke (schön)
c) Kevin is **doing an exercise.**	[ˈduːɪŋ_ən_ˈeksəsaɪz]	Kevin macht eine Übung.
exercise book	[ˈeksəsaɪz ˌbʊk]	Übungsheft
full	[fʊl]	voll
d) **this** question	[ˈðɪs ˈkwestʃən]	diese Frage (hier)
difficult	[ˈdɪfɪkəlt]	schwierig, schwer
easy	[ˈiːzɪ]	leicht, einfach
to see	[siː]	sehen

Exercises

1	**why**	[waɪ]	warum
4	**twenty**	[ˈtwentɪ]	zwanzig
	to work	[wɜːk]	arbeiten

Step 3 Behind the door

b) **the Kleins' house**		das Haus der Kleins
on the right	[ɒn ðə ˈraɪt]	rechts, auf der rechten Seite
on the left	[ɒn ðə ˈleft]	links, auf der linken Seite
to open	[ˈəʊpən]	öffnen
°**handle**	[ˈhændl]	°Klinke, Griff
only	[ˈəʊnlɪ]	nur
c) °**exciting**	[ɪkˈsaɪtɪŋ]	°aufregend
to look in	[ˌlʊk_ˈɪn]	hineinschauen
stairs	[steəz]	Treppen
°**attic**	[ˈætɪk]	°Dachboden
d) He **cannot climb through.**	[ˈkænɒt klaɪm ˈθruː]	Er kann nicht hindurchklettern.
to climb		klettern
through		durch, hindurch
He is **too big.**	[tuː ˈbɪg]	Er ist zu groß.
small	[smɔːl]	klein
to put	[pʊt]	stellen
here	[hɪə]	hierher
to stand	[stænd]	stehen
e) **dark**	[dɑːk]	dunkel
°**treasure**	[ˈtreʒə]	°Schatz
to come down	[ˌkʌm ˈdaʊn]	herunterkommen
f) **to get out**	[ˌget ˈaʊt]	herauskommen
high	[haɪ]	hoch
Let's all **push.**	[pʊʃ]	Laßt uns alle drücken.
to pull	[pʊl]	ziehen
g) °**to kick**	[kɪk]	°treten (gegen)
because	[bɪˈkɒz]	weil
angry	[ˈæŋgrɪ]	wütend, verärgert
h) °**bang!**	[bæŋ]	°peng! bums!
open	[ˈəʊpən]	offen, auf
up there	[ʌp ˈðeə]	dort oben
to look for	[ˈlʊk fɔː]	suchen

Exercises

2	**Who** can you see?	[huː]		Wen kannst du sehen?
7	°**opposite**	[ˈɒpəzɪt]		°Gegenteil, Gegensatz
8	**cardigan**	[ˈkɑːdɪgən]		Strickjacke

The Alphabet
°alphabet [ˈælfəbet] °Alphabet
°to spell [spel] °buchstabieren
°secret [ˈsiːkrɪt] °Geheimnis

⟨**Authentic Britain: Signs**⟩

sign [saɪn] Zeichen

Unit 4

Step 1 Tangram puzzles

°**Tangram puzzle**	[ˈtæŋgrəm ˈpʌzl]	*Name eines chinesischen Puzzles*
piece	[piːs]	Stück
°**bridge**	[brɪdʒ]	°Brücke
horse	[hɔːs]	Pferd
These are bridges.	[ˈðiːz‿ə ˈbrɪdʒɪz]	Dies (diese) hier sind Brücken
these		diese hier
Those are houses.	[ˈðəʊz‿ə ˈhaʊzɪz]	Das da sind Häuser.
those		diese dort
us	[ʌs]	uns
duck	[dʌk]	Ente
to swim	[swɪm]	schwimmen
hen	[hen]	Huhn, Henne
children	[ˈtʃɪldrən]	Kinder
men	[men]	Männer
to ride	[raɪd]	reiten
football	[ˈfʊtbɔːl]	Fußball
women	[ˈwɪmɪn]	Frauen
to dance	[dɑːns]	tanzen

Exercises

1	**picture-book**	[ˈpɪktʃəbʊk]	Bilderbuch
2	**child**	[tʃaɪld]	Kind
	°**lady (ladies)**	[ˈleɪdɪ]	°Dame (Damen)

Step 2 Over and out

Over and out.	[ˈəʊvər‿ən‿ˈaʊt]	Ende der Durchsage. *(Funksprache)*
Ronny can **talk to them.**	[ˈrɒnɪ kən ˈtɔːk tə ðəm]	Ronny kann mit ihnen reden.
to talk		reden, sprechen
them		sie, ihnen
by radio	[baɪ ˈreɪdɪəʊ]	per Funk
radio		Radio, Rundfunkgerät

Unit 4

to answer the telephone		das Telefon beantworten
when	[wen]	wenn
just now	[dʒʌst 'naʊ]	gerade jetzt
to send	[send]	schicken
I must be at the station at nine o'clock.	[aɪ 'mʌst bɪ‿ət ðə 'steɪʃn]	Ich muß um 9 Uhr am Bahnhof sein.
to be	[biː]	sein
What's your address?	[ə'dres]	Wie lautet Ihre Adresse?
Just a minute.	['dʒʌst‿ə 'mɪnɪt]	Einen Augenblick.
Come in, please.	[ˌkʌm ‿'ɪn]	Bitte melden! *(Funksprache)*
to hear	[hɪə]	hören
Over.	['əʊvə]	Ende. *(Funksprache)*
dad	[dæd]	Vati
to collect	[kə'lekt]	abholen
Can you **take her** to the station?	[teɪk hɜː]	Kannst du sie zum Bahnhof bringen?
to take		nehmen, bringen
her		sie, ihr
I've got (= I have got)	[aɪv 'gɒt]	Ich habe
passenger	['pæsɪndʒə]	Fahrgast, Passagier
I'm taking him to Tadcaster.	[aɪm 'teɪkɪŋ hɪm tə 'tædkɑːstə]	Ich bringe ihn (gerade) nach Tadcaster.
him		ihn, ihm
Tadcaster	['tædkɑːstə]	*Städtchen bei York*
perhaps	[pə'hæps]	vielleicht
hotel	[həʊ'tel]	Hotel
you	[juː]	Ihnen, euch, dich, dir
nobody	['nəʊbɒdɪ]	niemand
to telephone	['telɪfəʊn]	anrufen, telefonieren (mit)

Exercises

2	story	['stɒːrɪ]	Geschichte
⟨4⟩	role play	['rəʊl ˌpleɪ]	Rollenspiel
	there	[ðeə]	dorthin
	I've got it.	[aɪv 'gɒt‿ɪt]	Ich hab's! Verstanden!
	I've (= I have)		

Step 3 The box in the attic

a)	at Barbara's house	[ət 'bɑːbrəz ˌhaʊs]	bei Barbara zu Hause
	to go out	[ˌgəʊ 'aʊt]	weggehen
	O.K. then.	[ðen]	Also dann (ist es) in Ordnung.
	Goodbye.	[ˌgʊd 'baɪ]	Auf Wiedersehen!
b)	The box is not easy to open.		Die Truhe geht nicht leicht auf.
	clothes	['kləʊðz]	Kleider, Kleidung
	very	['verɪ]	sehr
	Never mind.	['nevə 'maɪnd]	Macht nichts!
	to take out	[ˌteɪk ‿'aʊt]	herausnehmen, herausholen
c)	Kate has got a **jacket** on.	['dʒækɪt]	Käte trägt ein Jackett.
	jacket		Jacke, Jackett
	°dress	[dres]	°Kleid

	coat	[kəʊt]	Mantel
	hat	[hæt]	Hut
	Not **bad**!	[bæd]	Nicht schlecht!
	bad		schlecht, schlimm
d)	**downstairs**	[ˈdaʊnˌsteəz]	unten, nach unten
	people	[ˈpiːpl]	Leute
e)	**Ssh!**		Sch(t)! Psst!
	someone	[ˈsʌmwʌn]	jemand
f)	Someone is coming		Jemand kommt nach oben.
	upstairs.	[ˌʌpˈsteəz]	Jemand kommt die Treppe herauf.
	to be afraid	[bɪ‿əˈfreɪd]	Angst haben
	to throw	[θrəʊ]	werfen
	head	[hed]	Kopf
	to push someone **onto** the floor	[ˈɒntʊ]	jemanden auf den Boden werfen
g)	**to sit up**	[ˌsɪt ˈʌp]	sich aufrichten

Exercises

2	**to give**	[gɪv]	geben
8	**class**	[klɑːs]	Klasse
⟨9⟩	to tell	[tel]	erzählen, berichten
	about	[əˈbaʊt]	von, über
10⟩	whole	[həʊl]	ganz
	world	[wɜːld]	Welt
	little bitty	[ˈlɪtl ˈbɪtɪ]	klitzeklein

Revision

> Mrs Pearson has got a sponge in **her** hand and a box under **her** arm.
> Kevin has got a water-pistol in **his** hand.
> You must throw a coat over **his** head, Ronny.
>
> Frau Pearson hat einen Schwamm in **der** Hand und einen Karton unter **dem** Arm.
> Kevin hat eine Wasserpistole in **der** Hand.
> Du mußt ihm einen Mantel über **den** Kopf werfen, Ronny.

Unit 5

⟨**Photo page: At the breakfast table**⟩

breakfast	[ˈbrekfəst]	Frühstück
often	[ˈɒfn]	oft
cornflakes	[ˈkɔːnfleɪks]	Cornflakes
toast	[təʊst]	Toast
marmalade	[ˈmɑːməleɪd]	Marmelade mit Zitrusfrüchten
bacon	[ˈbeɪkn]	Frühstücksspeck
egg	[eg]	Ei
sausage	[ˈsɒsɪdʒ]	Würstchen
for breakfast		zum Frühstück

Unit 5

Step 1 Numbers

thirteen	[ˈθɜːtiːn]	dreizehn
fourteen	[ˈfɔːtiːn]	vierzehn
fifteen	[ˈfɪftiːn]	fünfzehn
seventeen	[ˈsevntiːn]	siebzehn
eighteen	[ˈeɪtiːn]	achtzehn
nineteen	[ˈnaɪntiːn]	neunzehn
twenty-one	[ˈtwentɪ ˈwʌn]	einundzwanzig
thirty	[ˈθɜːtɪ]	dreißig
forty	[ˈfɔːtɪ]	vierzig
fifty	[ˈfɪftɪ]	fünfzig
eighty	[ˈeɪtɪ]	achtzig
a/one hundred	[ə/wʌn ˈhʌndrəd]	hundert

Exercises

1 bus — [bʌs] — Bus
   to get to — — gelangen, kommen

Step 2 The bus driver

Wheldrake	[ˈweldreɪk]	*Dörfer in der*
Escrick	[ˈeskrɪk]	*Umgebung*
Stillingfleet	[ˈstɪlɪŋfliːt]	*von York*
°reporter	[rɪˈpɔːtə]	°Reporter, Reporterin
about	[əˈbaʊt]	über, von
job	[dʒɒb]	Arbeit, Job
a) bus driver	[ˈbʌs ˈdraɪvə]	Busfahrer(-in)
village	[ˈvɪlɪdʒ]	Dorf
every morning	[ˈevrɪ ˈmɔːnɪŋ]	jeden Morgen
every		jeder, jede, jedes
to get up	[ˌget ˈʌp]	aufstehen
early	[ˈɜːlɪ]	früh
I start at half past seven.	[aɪ ˌstɑːt ət ˈhɑːf ˌpɑːst ˈsevn]	Ich fange um halb acht an.
to start		anfangen
half past seven		halb acht
to get to school	[ˌget tə ˈskuːl]	die Schule erreichen, zur Schule kommen
quarter to nine	[ˈkwɔːtə tə ˈnaɪn]	viertel vor neun, dreiviertel neun
again	[əˈgen]	wieder, noch einmal
to come out	[ˌkʌm ˈaʊt]	herauskommen
I take the children home.	[həʊm]	Ich bringe die Kinder nach Hause.
Well, no.		Eigentlich nicht.
often	[ˈɒfn]	oft
thing	[θɪŋ]	Sache, Ding
b) the next day	[deɪ]	am nächsten Tag
to want	[wɒnt]	wollen, mögen
to hold	[həʊld]	halten, abhalten, veranstalten
°jumble sale	[ˈdʒʌmbl seɪl]	(eine Art) °Flohmarkt (für Wohltätigkeitszwecke)

Unit 5

Now I want to hold a °jumble sale.   Nun möchte ich einen Flohmarkt veranstalten.

Exercises

G	They **mustn't** be late for school.	['mʌsnt]	Sie dürfen nicht zu spät zur Schule kommen.
	on Sundays	['sʌndeɪz]	sonntags
3	**What time is it,** please?	[wɒt 'taɪm ɪz ɪt]	Wie spät ist es bitte?
	time		Zeit, Uhrzeit
4	You can **also** say…	['ɔːlsəʊ]	Du kannst auch sagen…
5	**Monday**	['mʌndeɪ]	Montag

Step 3   Kate's kite

kite	[kaɪt]	Drachen
park	[pɑːk]	Park
to teach a dog a trick	['tiːtʃ ə dɒg ə 'trɪk]	einem Hund ein Kunststück beibringen
to teach		unterrichten, lehren, beibringen
trick		Kunststück, Trick
stick	[stɪk]	Stock
The dog **runs after** the stick.	['ɑːftə]	Der Hund rennt hinter dem Stock her.
to pick up	[ˌpɪk 'ʌp]	aufheben
back	[bæk]	zurück
biscuit	['bɪskɪt]	Keks, *hier:* Hundekuchen
Good boy.		*hier:* Braver Hund.
she holds the **string**	[strɪŋ]	sie hält die Schnur, Kordel
to fly	[flaɪ]	fliegen
into the **air**	[eə]	in die Luft
to fall down	[ˌfɔːl 'daʊn]	herunterfallen, hinfallen
to run away	[ˌrʌn ə'weɪ]	weglaufen
°hole	[həʊl]	°Loch
The man **is** very **sorry**.	['sɒri]	Es tut dem Mann sehr leid.

Exercises

1	**Put** the sentences **together**.		Setzt die Sätze zusammen.
4	**ball**	[bɒl]	Ball

Step 4   Bonzo the dog

pet	[pet]	Haustier, Liebling
to wake someone up	[weɪk]	jemanden wecken
to wash	[wɒʃ]	waschen
face	[feɪs]	Gesicht
breakfast	['brekfəst]	Frühstück
after that	['ɑːftə 'ðæt]	danach, anschließend
to have breakfast		frühstücken
always	['ɔːlweɪz]	immer
to get lost	[ˌget 'lɒst]	sich verirren, sich verlaufen
to shout	[ʃaʊt]	rufen
lunch	[lʌntʃ]	Mittagessen

one hundred and fifty-seven

Unit 5/Unit 6

over the wall		über die Mauer
to bark (at someone)	[bɑ:k]	(jemanden an)bellen
for example	[fər‿ɪgˈzɑ:mpl]	zum Beispiel
to bring	[brɪŋ]	bringen
to ride away	[ˌraɪd əˈweɪ]	wegfahren (auf dem Fahrrad)
bike	[baɪk]	Fahrrad
the **other** cars	[ðɪ‿ˈʌðə ˌkɑ:z]	die anderen Autos
tea	[ti:]	Tee, Teestunde, Abendbrot
to like	[laɪk]	mögen
I take Peter **to bed**.	[tə ˈbed]	*hier:* Ich nehme Peter mit ins Bett. (Ich bringe ihn ins Bett.)
He's a **good** boy.		Er ist ein braver Junge.
to sleep	[sli:p]	schlafen

Exercises

3	when	[wen]	wann
4	°church	[tʃɜ:tʃ]	°Kirche
5	week	[wi:k]	Woche
	Tuesday	[ˈtju:zdeɪ]	Dienstag
	Wednesday	[ˈwenzdeɪ]	Mittwoch
	Thursday	[ˈθɜ:zdeɪ]	Donnerstag
	Friday	[ˈfraɪdeɪ]	Freitag
⟨7⟩	music man	[ˈmju:zɪk ˈmæn]	Musikant
	violin	[ˈvaɪəlɪn]	Violine
	bicycle	[ˈbaɪsɪkl]	Fahrrad
8	A good dog comes when you shout **its** name.	[ɪts]	Ein braver Hund kommt, wenn du seinen Namen rufst.

Revision

> **bringen**
>
> Wendy **takes** the children home. Wendy **bringt** die Kinder nach Hause.
> Mr Bennett **is taking** a passenger to the station. Herr Bennett **bringt** gerade einen Fahrgast zum Bahnhof.
>
> When Bonzo **brings** a stick, the boys throw it away again. Wenn Bonzo einen Stock **herbringt**, werfen ihn die Jungen wieder weg.
> "**Bring** me an empty box, please." „Bitte **bring** mir eine leere Schachtel."

Unit 6

⟨**Photo page: Whitby**⟩

Whitby	[ˈwɪtbɪ]	*Stadt an der Küste in Yorkshire*
harbour	[ˈhɑ:bə]	Hafen
sands	[sændz]	Sandstrand
bay	[beɪ]	Bucht

Step 1 By train to Whitby

by train to Whitby	[baɪ ˈtreɪn]	mit dem Zug nach Whitby
Whitby	[ˈwɪtbɪ]	*Stadt an der Küste in Yorkshire*

158 *one hundred and fifty-eight*

Unit 6

a) **plan** [plæn] Plan
picnic ['pɪknɪk] Picknick
to go to the **seaside** ['siːsaɪd] ans Meer fahren
°**Railway Museum** ['reɪlweɪ mjuːˈzɪəm] °Eisenbahnmuseum
to fly [flaɪ] fliegen lassen
b) **to tell** [tel] erzählen, berichten
different ['dɪfrənt] verschieden, unterschiedlich
by bus [baɪ ˈbʌs] mit dem Bus
Pickering ['pɪkrɪŋ] *Städtchen in Yorkshire*
on the **beach** [biːtʃ] am Strand
happy ['hæpɪ] glücklich
everybody ['evrɪbɒdɪ] jeder
c) **to cry** [kraɪ] weinen
What's the matter? ['mætə] Was ist los?
to look after someone [ˌlʊk ˈɑːftə] auf jemanden aufpassen

Exercises

1 **to think** [θɪŋk] denken, meinen, glauben
2 **next** [nekst] als nächstes, dann
3 **letter** ['letə] Brief
wait a minute ['weɪt ə 'mɪnɪt] Augenblick mal!

Step 2 Picnic food

°**food** [fuːd] °Essen, Nahrung
banana [bəˈnɑːnə] Banane
orange ['ɒrɪndʒ] Apfelsine
apple ['æpl] Apfel
sandwich ['sænwɪdʒ] Sandwich, Butterbrot
a packet of biscuits [ˌpækɪt əv 'bɪskɪts] eine Packung Kekse
a bag of sweets [ˌbæg əv 'swiːts] eine Tüte Bonbons
sweets Süßigkeiten, Bonbons
a glass of milk [ˌglɑːs əv 'mɪlk] ein Glas Milch
a bottle of lemonade [ˌbɒtl əv ˌleməˈneɪd] eine Flasche Limonade
a bar of chocolate [ˌbɑːr əv 'tʃɒklət] eine Tafel Schokolade
b) I'm **hungry**. ['hʌŋgrɪ] Ich habe Hunger.
hungry hungrig
Have a biscuit. Nimm/Nehmt einen Keks.
I'm **thirsty**. ['θɜːstɪ] Ich habe Durst.
thirsty durstig
Sorry, it's °**all gone**. [ˌɔːl 'gɒn] Tut mir leid, es ist °alles weg.

Exercises

2 **role play** ['rəʊl ˌpleɪ] Rollenspiel
here you are [ˌhɪə juː 'ɑː] Bitteschön.
3 **plastic bag** [ˌplæstɪk 'bæg] Plastiktüte
bag Tasche, Tüte
to cut [kʌt] schneiden
to tie [taɪ] befestigen, (an)binden
ready ['redɪ] fertig

Unit 6

Step 3 Seaside Special

°special	['speʃl]	*hier:* °Sondersendung
a) poor	[pʊə]	arm
unhappy	[ʌn'hæpɪ]	unglücklich
b) bus station	['bʌs ˌsteɪʃn]	Busbahnhof
to get into	[ˌget 'ɪntʊ]	einsteigen
°smoke	[sməʊk]	°Rauch
to laugh at someone	[lɑːf]	jemanden auslachen
c) They **get out of** the train.		Sie steigen aus dem Zug aus.
sea	[siː]	Meer
She starts **to run.**		Sie fängt an zu laufen.
She falls over a **stone.**	[stəʊn]	Sie fällt über einen Stein.
to break	[breɪk]	zerbrechen, kaputtgehen
d) windy	['wɪndɪ]	windig
e) an hour later	[ən 'aʊə 'leɪtə]	eine Stunde später
warm	[wɔːm]	warm
when	[wen]	als
blue **with cold**		blau vor Kälte
to put on	[ˌpʊt 'ɒn]	anziehen
BBC	[ˌbiː biː 'siː]	*britischer Rundfunk- und Fernsehsender*
What's happening?	[ˌwɒts 'hæpnɪŋ]	Was ist los?
to happen	['hæpn]	geschehen, passieren
f) °request	[rɪ'kwest]	°(Platten-)Wunsch, Bitte
somebody	['sʌmbɒdɪ]	(irgend)jemand

Exercises

3	It's too **cold**	[kəʊld]	Es ist zu kalt.
4	to walk	[wɔːk]	zu Fuß gehen
G	°at playtime	[ət 'pleɪtaɪm]	°in der Pause
7	What's the weather like?	[ˌwɒts ðə 'weðə ˌlaɪk]	Wie ist das Wetter?
	weather		Wetter
	British	['brɪtɪʃ]	britisch
⟨8⟩	Hip, hip, hip hurray.	['hɪp 'hɪp 'hɪp hʊ'reɪ]	Hipp hipp, hurra!
	gay	[geɪ]	fröhlich, lustig
	Today's a holiday.	['hɒlɪdeɪ]	Heute ist ein Feiertag.

⟨**Authentic Britain: Moorsrail**⟩

Moorsrail	['mʊəzreɪl]	*Name einer privaten Eisenbahngesellschaft*

Revision

Zeit- und Häufigkeitsadverbien			
always	immer	first	zuerst
again	wieder	after that	danach
every morning	jeden Morgen	next	als nächstes
often	oft	the next day	am nächsten Tag
sometimes	manchmal	then	dann
		at last	endlich

Unit 7

⟨Photo page: Houses in Britain⟩

terraced house	[terəst]	Reihenhaus
semi-detached house	[ˌsemɪdɪˈtætʃt]	Doppelhaushälfte
detached house	[dɪˈtætʃt]	Einzelhaus

Step 1 The 'Twenty Questions' Game

to think of something	[ˈθɪŋk‿əv]	an etwas denken
the **others**	[ðɪ‿ˈʌðəz]	die anderen
°**to guess**	[ges]	°raten
for an answer		als Antwort
It is Ronny's **turn**.	[tɜ:n]	Ronny ist an der Reihe.
to **eat**	[i:t]	essen
useful	[ˈju:sfʊl]	nützlich
not really	[ˌnɒt ˈrɪəlɪ]	eigentlich nicht
Do I **use** it?	[du:]	Benutze ich es?
No, you **don't**.	[dəʊnt]	Nein.
to **use**	[ju:z]	benutzen, verwenden
Five questions **gone**.	[gɒn]	Fünf Fragen weg.
to **buy**	[baɪ]	kaufen
to **sell**	[sel]	verkaufen
Hands up!	[ˈhændz‿ˈʌp]	Hände hoch!
Hooray!	[hʊˈreɪ]	Hurra!
...**just** when I'm **winning**.	[ˈdʒʌst wen aɪm ˈwɪnɪŋ]	...gerade jetzt, wo ich gewinne!
to **win**		gewinnen

Exercises

2	**to know**	[nəʊ]	wissen, kennen

Step 2 All about Kevin

1	**before** tea	[bɪˈfɔ:]	vor dem Abendessen
3	**usually**	[ˈju:ʒwəlɪ]	gewöhnlich, normalerweise
	for breakfast	[fɔ: ˈbrekfəst]	zum Frühstück
	cornflakes	[ˈkɔ:nfleɪks]	Cornflakes
	egg	[eg]	Ei
	two pieces of bread	[tʊ ˈpi:sɪz‿əv ˈbred]	zwei Scheiben Brot
	butter	[ˈbʌtə]	Butter
	bacon	[ˈbeɪkn]	Frühstücksspeck
	a piece of toast	[əˌpi:s‿əv ˈtəʊst]	eine Scheibe Toast
	marmalade	[ˈmɑ:məleɪd]	Marmelade mit Zitrusfrüchten
	a cup of tea	[əˌkʌp‿əv ˈti:]	eine Tasse Tee
	roll	[rəʊl]	Brötchen
	cheese	[tʃi:z]	Käse
	sausage	[ˈsɒsɪdʒ]	Wurst
	coffee	[ˈkɒfɪ]	Kaffee
4	**dining-room**	[ˈdaɪnɪŋ rʊm]	Eßzimmer
	kitchen	[ˈkɪtʃɪn]	Küche
5	**to visit**	[ˈvɪsɪt]	besuchen

Unit 7

Do you want **another** cup of tea?	[əˈnʌðə]	Möchtest du noch eine Tasse Tee?
more toast?	[mɔː ˈtəʊst]	noch ein Toastbrot?

Step 3   Upstairs and Downstairs

hall	[hɔːl]	Flur, Diele
to miss one turn	[ˈmɪs wʌn ˌtɜːn]	eine Runde aussetzen
to sit down	[ˌsɪt ˈdaʊn]	sich setzen
to wash up	[ˌwɒʃ ˈʌp]	spülen, abwaschen
… until you throw a six.	[ənˈtɪl]	… bis du eine Sechs wirfst.
sitting-room	[ˈsɪtɪŋ rʊm]	Wohnzimmer
Take an °**extra** turn.	[ˈekstrə]	*hier:* °Du darfst noch einmal würfeln.
to go to bed		ins Bett gehen
to have a bath	[bɑːθ]	baden
to know	[nəʊ]	kennen, wissen
Does Kevin know it?	[dʌz]	Kennt es Kevin? –
No, he **doesn't**.	[ˈdʌznt]	Nein.
everyone	[ˈevrɪwʌn]	jeder(mann), alle
°**counter**	[ˈkaʊntə]	°Spielmarke
°**dice**	[daɪs]	°Würfel
front door	[ˌfrʌnt ˈdɔː]	Eingangstür
back door	[ˌbæk ˈdɔː]	Hintertür
to end	[end]	enden
to mean	[miːn]	bedeuten
bad luck	[ˌbæd ˈlʌk]	Pech
Ugh!	[ɜːh]	i! i gitt!
of course	[əv ˈkɔːs]	natürlich
°**winner**	[ˈwɪnə]	°Sieger(in), Gewinner(in)
No, not again		Nein, nicht noch einmal./Nein, nicht schon wieder.
Why not?		Warum nicht?
silly	[ˈsɪlɪ]	albern, dumm, doof
That's why.	[ˈðæts ˈwaɪ]	Deshalb

Revision

In the house			
house	Haus	**bathroom**	Badezimmer
flat	Wohnung	°**attic**	Dachboden
(front) door	(Haus)tür	**stairs**	Treppe
back door	Tür (hinter dem Haus)	**wall**	Wand, Mauer
window	Fenster	**floor**	Fußboden
hall	Flur, Diele	**cupboard**	Schrank
sitting-room	Wohnzimmer	**bed**	Bett
dining-room	Eßzimmer	**chair**	Stuhl
kitchen	Küche	**table**	Tisch
bedroom	Schlafzimmer	°**handle**	Griff, Klinke

Exercises

G	**to drink**	[drɪŋk]	trinken
5	**outside**	[ˌaʊtˈsaɪd]	draußen
6	**to live**	[lɪv]	leben

Unit 7 – Fun Pages 1/2

town	[taʊn]	Stadt
⟨8⟩ if	[ɪf]	wenn, falls
Clap your hands.	[klæp]	Klatsche in die Hände!
action	[ˈækʃn]	*hier:* Bewegung
surely	[ˈʃɔːlɪ]	sicherlich
to show	[ʃəʊ]	zeigen
Stamp your feet.	[stæmp]	Stampfe mit den Füßen!
Snap your fingers.	[snæp]	Schnippe mit den Fingern!

Fun Pages 1

°fun	[fʌn]	°Spaß

1 Circus in York

°circus	[ˈsɜːkəs]	°Zirkus
°elephant	[ˈelɪfənt]	°Elefant

2 The hungry elephant

°elephant	[ˈelɪfənt]	°Elefant
°caravan	[ˈkærəvæn]	°Wohnwagen
°trunk	[trʌnk]	°Rüssel
°What a **mess**.	[ˈwɒt‿əˈmes]	°Was für ein Durcheinander! Wie sieht's denn hier aus!

Fun Pages 2

1 On holiday

on holiday	[ɒn ˈhɒlɪdeɪ]	in den Ferien
School is **over**.	[ˈəʊvə]	Die Schule ist aus.
°to stay	[steɪ]	°bleiben
°for a week	[fɔːr‿ə ˈwiːk]	°eine Woche (lang).
°cousin	[ˈkʌzn]	°Cousin, Cousine
°farm	[fɑːm]	°Bauernhof, Farm
° Scotland	[ˈskɒtlənd]	°Schottland
°American	[əˈmerɪkən]	°Amerikaner, -in amerikanisch
°tourist	[ˈtʊərɪst]	°Tourist, Touristin
°to show	[ʃəʊ]	°zeigen
°She shows them **round** York.	[raʊnd]	°Sie führt sie in York herum/ durch York.

2 Role play

°hobby	[ˈhɒbɪ]	°Freizeitbeschäftigung; Hobby
°some	[sʌm]	°einige

3 A letter-puzzle

°to put in the right **order**	[ˈɔːdə]	°in die richtige Reihenfolge bringen
°lovely	[ˈlʌvlɪ]	°schön
Uncle Jim	[ˈʌŋkl]	Onkel Jim
°farm	[fɑːm]	°Bauernhof, Farm
°tractor	[ˈtræktə]	°Traktor, Trecker
°to jump	[dʒʌmp]	°springen

°near… [nɪə] °in der Nähe von…
°chips [tʃɪps] °Pommes frites

Fun Pages 3

°magic ['mædʒɪk] °Zauber, Zauberei
°joke [dʒəʊk] °Witz

1 How many
°group [gru:p] °Gruppe

2 It's magic
°to show [ʃəʊ] °zeigen
°a secret letter ['si:krɪt 'letə] °ein geheimer Brief
°a piece of paper ['peɪpə] °ein Stück Papier
°dry [draɪ] °trocken
°to understand [ˌʌndə'stænd] °verstehen
°candle ['kændl] °Kerze
°soon [su:n] °bald
°to look brown [ˌlʊk 'braʊn] °braun aussehen

4 Kim's Game
°birthday party ['bɜ:θdeɪ 'pɑ:tɪ] °Geburtstagsfeier
°to write down [ˌraɪt 'daʊn] °aufschreiben
°to shut [ʃʌt] °zumachen, schließen
°to remember [rɪ'membə] °erinnern

5 The magic matchbox
°matchbox ['mætʃbɒks] °Streichholzschachtel
°coin [kɔɪn] °Münze
°lid [lɪd] °Deckel
°finger ['fɪŋgə] °Finger
°end [end] °Ende

6 A joke
°rabbit ['ræbɪt] °Kaninchen

Additum Unit 5

2 What the Pearsons do every day
to buy [baɪ] kaufen

3 Wendy's day
Say what happens every day ['hæpənz] Sag was jeden Tag geschieht.

4 A day with Bonzo
Tell the story ['stɔ:rɪ] Erzähle die Geschichte.

6 The mysterious piano player
mysterious [mɪ'stɪərɪəs] geheimnisvoll
piano player [pɪ'ænəʊ ˌpleɪə] Klavierspieler
music ['mju:zɪk] Musik

Additum Unit 5/Unit 6

piano lesson	[ˈlesn]	Klavierstunde
not ... yet	[jet]	noch nicht
neighbour	[ˈneɪbə]	Nachbar
key	[kiː]	Schlüssel, *hier:* Taste
happy	[ˈhæpɪ]	glücklich
little Jane	[ˌlɪtl ˈdʒeɪn]	die kleine Jane
noise	[nɔɪz]	Lärm
to jump	[dʒʌmp]	springen
to switch on/off	[ˌswɪtʃ ˈɒn/ˈɒf]	an-/ausschalten
light	[laɪt]	Licht
sitting-room	[ˈsɪtɪŋ rʊm]	Wohnzimmer
to be asleep	[əˈsliːp]	schlafen
Are her parents **back**?	[bæk]	Sind ihre Eltern zurück?
kitchen	[ˈkɪtʃɪn]	Küche
suddenly	[ˈsʌdnlɪ]	plötzlich

7 The clown in the box

Tell the story.	[ˈstɔːrɪ]	Erzähle die Geschichte
clown	[klaʊn]	Clown
to show	[ʃəʊ]	zeigen
to lock	[lɒk]	verschließen
to put down	[ˌpʊt ˈdaʊn]	hinstellen
to sit down	[ˌsɪt ˈdaʊn]	sich setzen

8 A letter from Barbara

letter	[ˈletə]	Brief
cornflakes	[ˈkɔːnfleɪks]	Cornflakes
milk	[mɪlk]	Milch
milkman	[ˈmɪlkmən]	Milchmann
bottle	[ˈbɒtl]	Flasche
to leave	[liːv]	verlassen, (weg)gehen
usually	[ˈjuːʒʊəlɪ]	gewöhnlich, normalerweise
love from...	[ˈlʌv frɒm]	viele liebe Grüße von...

9 Listening comprehension

to fetch	[fetʃ]	holen
what happens	[wɒt ˈhæpənz]	was passiert?
second	[ˈsekənd]	der/die/das zweite
third	[θɜːd]	der/die/das dritte

Additum Unit 6

1 On time

on time	[ɒn ˈtaɪm]	pünktlich
clock	[klɒk]	Uhr
exact	[ɪɡˈzækt]	genau

2 How they get to school every morning

to walk	[wɔːk]	laufen, zu Fuß gehen
His train **arrives** at the station...	[əˈraɪvz]	Sein Zug kommt am Bahnhof an...

Additum Unit 6

3 Timetables

timetable	[ˈtaɪmˌteɪbl]	Fahrplan
Levisham	[ˈlevɪʃəm]	*Dörfer an der Bahnlinie Moorsrail*
Goathland	[ˈgəʊθlənd]	
Grosmont	[ˈgrəʊsmənt]	
to leave	[liːv]	*hier:* abfahren
to arrive at	[əˈraɪv]	ankommen

4 Early, late, on time

early	[ˈɜːlɪ]	*hier:* zu früh
on time	[ɒn ˈtaɪm]	pünktlich
A train is **arriving** at Grosmont.	[əˈraɪvɪŋ]	In Grosmont kommt soeben ein Zug an.

5 Say what you do

usually	[ˈjuːʒʊəlɪ]	gewöhnlich, normalerweise
to watch	[wɒtʃ]	beachten
word order	[ˈwɜːd ˌɔːdə]	Wortstellung
cornflakes	[ˈkɔːnfleɪks]	Cornflakes

6 After school

I **take off** my school uniform.	[ˌteɪk ˈɒf]	Ich ziehe meine Schuluniform aus.
usually	[ˈjuːʒʊəlɪ]	gewöhnlich, normalerweise
to fetch	[fetʃ]	holen
a bit	[ə ˈbɪt]	ein wenig
he does	[dʌz]	er macht

7 Making plans

Let's **sing some songs**.	[lets ˈsɪŋ səm ˈsɒŋz]	Laßt uns einige Lieder singen.

8 Fizz

I understand	[ˌʌndəˈstænd]	Ich verstehe

11 Listening comprehension

Scarborough	[ˈskaːbərə]	*Seebad an der Küste von Yorkshire*
to live	[lɪv]	leben, wohnen
Who is it for?	[ˈhuː ɪz ɪt ˈfɔː]	Für wen ist es?

12 In the snack-bar

snack-bar	[ˈsnæk baː]	Imbißstube
self service	[ˈself ˈsɜːvɪs]	Selbstbedienung
the door opens		die Tür geht auf, die Tür öffnet sich
tray	[treɪ]	Tablett
a piece of **cake**	[ˈkeɪk]	ein Stück Kuchen
yoghurt	[ˈjɒgət]	Joghurt
cash desk	[ˈkæʃ desk]	Kasse
to begin	[bɪˈgɪn]	anfangen

13 All about me

Talk about **yourself**.	[jɔːˈself]	Sprich über dich (selbst).

Additum Unit 7

1 Elke and Jane

Heslington	[ˈhezlɪŋtən]	*Ortsname*
if	[ɪf]	ob

2 Role play

I don't mind.	[aɪ dəʊnt ˈmaɪnd]	Es ist mir egal.
Oh no, not again.	[ˈnɒt ə'gen]	Nein, nicht schon wieder.

3 Sunday afternoon out

to have a good time	[ˈhæv ə gʊd ˈtaɪm]	viel Spaß haben
to forget	[fəˈget]	vergessen
nice	[naɪs]	nett, hübsch
to call	[kɔːl]	rufen
bus stop	[ˈbʌs stɒp]	Bushaltestelle
castle	[ˈkɑːsl]	Burg
interesting	[ˈɪntrəstɪŋ]	interessant
street	[striːt]	Straße
to leave	[liːv]	verlassen
sweet shop	[ˈswiːt ʃɒp]	Süßwarenladen
so wonderful	[səʊ ˈwʌndəfʊl]	so hübsch
to walk back	[ˌwɔːk ˈbæk]	zurücklaufen
far	[fɑː]	weit
to look out of the window	[lʊk ˈaʊt əv ðə ˈwɪndəʊ]	zum Fenster hinausschauen
to get off	[ˌget ˈɒf]	aussteigen (aus einem Bus/Zug)
seat	[siːt]	Sitz(platz)
to stop	[stɒp]	anhalten
at the bus stop		an der Bushaltestelle
at last	[ət ˈlɑːst]	endlich!
on his way back	[ɒn hɪz weɪ ˈbæk]	auf dem Rückweg
river	[ˈrɪvə]	Fluß
watch	[wɒtʃ]	Armbanduhr
to get back		zurückkommen
the only way	[ðɪ ˈəʊnlɪ ˈweɪ]	der einzige Weg, die einzige Möglichkeit
to ring up	[ˌrɪŋ ˈʌp]	anrufen
Timmy is **gone**	[gɒn]	Timmy ist verschwunden
round the house	[raʊnd]	um das Haus (herum)
voice	[vɔɪs]	Stimme
doorstep	[ˈdɔːstep]	Stufe vor der Tür
to look unhappy	[ˌlʊk ʌnˈhæpɪ]	unglücklich aussehen
not...at all	[nɒt ət ˈɔːl]	überhaupt nicht

4 Comprehension

alone	[əˈləʊn]	allein

6 Listening comprehension

Newcastle	[ˈnjuːkɑːsl]	*Industriestadt im Nordosten Englands*

Alphabetical Word List

- Die Zahlen verweisen auf das erstmalige Vorkommen der Wörter, z. B.
  bus 5 1 69,1 = Unit 5, Step 1, Seite 69, Übung 1
  arm FS 7 20,b) = First Scenes 7, Seite 20, Pararaph b)
  alone Add 7 118,4 = Additum zu Unit 7, Seite 118, Übung 4
  °**candle FP 3** 104,2 = Fun Pages 3, Seite 104, Übung 2
- Das Zeichen ° vor einer Angabe bedeutet, daß das Wort zum rezeptiven Wortschatz zählt.
- Das Zeichen 〈 〉 vor einer Angabe weist darauf hin, daß das Wort fakultativ ist.
- Um einen möglichst umfassenden Wortschatzüberblick zu gewährleisten, sind Wendungen, die sich aus verschiedenen Komponenten zusammensetzen, unter mehreren Stichwörtern aufgeführt. So ist z. B. *at home* unter *home* und *at* zu finden.

A

a	ein, eine	**FS 5** 14,a)	**at**			
〈to talk about	sprechen über	4 3 67,9〉	to laugh at	auslachen	6 3 85,b)
to talk **about**	sprechen über	5 2 70	to look at	anschauen	**FS 3** 10,a)
What about...?	Wie ist es mit...?	1 2 31,1	not ... at all	überhaupt nicht	**Add 7** 117.3
〈action	Handlung	7 3 99,8〉	at home	zu Hause	**FS 9** 26,a)
address	Anschrift	4 2 60	at last	endlich	**Add 7** 116,3
afraid			at night	nachts	**FS 9** 26,a)
to be afraid	Angst haben	4 3 64,f)	at school	in der Schule	**FS 9** 26,a)
after			at the bus stop	an der Bushaltestelle	**Add 7** 116,3
after that	danach	5 4 75	at the Kleins' house	bei den Kleins	3 3 51,b)
to look after someone	auf jdn aufpassen	6 1 81,c)	at the window	am Fenster	1 1 29,b)
to run after	hinterherrennen	5 3 73	°**attic**	Dachboden	3 3 51,c)
afternoon	Nachmittag	**FS 9** 26,a)	〈**authentic**	echt, authentisch	1 *Authentic Britain* 35〉
again	wieder	5 2 70,a)	**away**		
not again	nicht schon wieder	**Add 6** 112,7	to run away	weglaufen	5 3 73
		7 3 96	to ride away	wegfahren (mit dem Fahrrad)	5 4 75
air	Luft	5 3 73			
all	alle	**FS 9** 26,a)	**B**		
°all gone	alles weg	6 2 83,b)	°**baby**	Baby	**FS 8** 23,b)
not ... at all	überhaupt nicht	**Add 7** 117,3	°baby brother	kleiner Bruder	**FS 8** 23,b)
alone	allein	**Add 7** 118,4	**back**	zurück	5 3 73
°**alphabet**	Alphabet	3 3 56	back door	Hintertür	7 3 96
also	auch	5 2 72,4	〈to bring back	zurückbringen	2 4 44,6〉
always	immer	5 4 75	to walk back	zurücklaufen	**Add 7** 116,3
I **am**	ich bin	**FS 4** 12,2	Are her parents back?	Sind ihre Eltern zurück?	**Add 5** 108,6
°**American**	Amerikaner, -in; amerikanisch	**FP 2** 102,1	〈**bacon**	Frühstücksspeck	5 *Photo page* 68〉
an	ein, eine	3 2 49,b)	**bacon**	Frühstücksspeck	7 2 95,3
and	und	**FS 2** 9	**bad**	schlecht	4 3 63,c)
angry	wütend	3 3 52,g)	bad luck	Pech	7 3 96
another	noch ein(e)	7 2 95,5	school-**bag**	Schultasche	1 3 33,c)
answer	Antwort	**FS 4** 12,1	a **bag** of sweets	eine Tüte Bonbons	6 2 83
for an answer	als Antwort	7 1 92	**ball**	Ball	5 3 74,4
to answer	beantworten	**FS 6** 18,2	**banana**	Banane	6 2 83
apple	Apfel	6 2 83	°**bang**	peng	3 3 52,h)
are	bist, seid, sind	**FS 2** 9,b)	a **bar** of chocolate	eine Tafel Schokolade	6 2 83
they aren't	sie sind nicht	**FS 6** 17,c)			
arm	Arm	**FS 7** 20,b)			
to **arrive** at	ankommen	**Add 6** 111,2			
to **ask**	fragen	**FS 5** 14,1			
to be **asleep**	schlafen	**Add 5** 108,6			

Alphabetical Word List

to **bark**	bellen	5 4 75
bath		
to have a bath	ein Bad nehmen	7 3 96
bathroom	Badezimmer	2 4 42
⟨**bay**	Bucht	6 *Photo page* 80⟩
to **be**	sein	4 2 60
be careful	sei vorsichtig	1 1 30,2
beach	Strand	6 1 81,b)
because	weil	3 3 52,g)
bed	Bett	FS 9 26,a)
to go to bed	ins Bett gehen	7 3 96
to take to bed	ins Bett bringen	5 4 76
bedroom	Schlafzimmer	3 2 49,a)
before	vor	7 2 94,1
⟨**bicycle**	Fahrrad	5 4 78,7⟩
to **begin**	anfangen	**Add 6** 114,12
behind	hinter	FS 7 21,c)
big	groß	3 3 51,d)
bike	Fahrrad	5 4 75
biro	Kugelschreiber	1 3 33,b)
°**birthday party**	Geburtstagsfeier	FP 3 105,4
biscuit	Hundekuchen	5 3 73
	Keks	6 2 83
a **bit**	ein wenig	**Add 6** 112,6
⟨**bitty**	klitzeklein	4 3 67,10⟩
black	schwarz	3 1 47
°**blazer**	Blazer	3 1 47
blouse	Bluse	3 1 47
blue	blau	3 1 47
blue with cold	blau vor Kälte	6 3 86,e)
book	Buch	1 2 31,b)
exercise book	Heft	3 2 49,c)
picture-book	Bilderbuch	4 1 59,1
bottle	Flasche	**Add 5** 109,8
		6 2 83
box	Karton, Schachtel	FS 7 20,b)
boy	Junge	FS 1 8,b)
bread	Brot	7 2 95,3
to **break**	zerbrechen	6 3 85,c)
⟨**breakfast**	Frühstück	5 *Photo page* 68⟩
⟨for breakfast	zum Frühstück	5 *Photo page* 68⟩
breakfast	Frühstück	5 4 75
to have breakfast	frühstücken	5 4 75
for breakfast	zum Frühstück	7 2 95,3
°**bridge**	Brücke	4 1 58
to **bring**	(her)bringen	5 4 75
⟨to bring back	zurückbringen	2 4 44,6⟩
⟨**Britain**	Großbritannien	1 *Authentic Britain* 35⟩
Britain	Großbritannien	3 1 47
⟨**British**	britisch	3 *Photo page* 46⟩
British	britisch	6 3 89,7
brother	Bruder	FS 5 14,b)
brown	braun	2 4 44,5

brush	Bürste, Besen	FS 7 20,b)
bucket	Eimer	FS 7 20,b)
bus	Bus	5 1 69,1
bus driver	Busfahrer(in)	5 2 70
bus station	Busbahnhof	6 3 85,b)
bus stop	Bushaltestelle	**Add 7** 116,3
by bus	mit dem Bus	6 1 81,b)
but	aber	FS 7 20,b)
butter	Butter	7 2 95,3
to **buy**	kaufen	**Add 5** 106,2
		7 1 92
by		
by bus	mit dem Bus	6 1 81,b)
by radio	per Funk	4 2 60
by train	mit dem Zug	6 1 81

C

cake	Kuchen	**Add 6** 114,12
to **call**	rufen	**Add 7** 116,3
can	können	1 2 31
cannot	nicht können	3 3 51,d)
can't	nicht können	1 2 31,1
°**candle**	Kerze	FP 3 104,2
car	Auto	1 1 29,a)
°**caravan**	Wohnwagen	FP 1 101,2
cardigan	Strickjacke	3 3 55,8
cards	Karten	2 4 42
careful	vorsichtig	1 1 30,2
be careful	sei vorsichtig	1 1 30,2
to **carry**	tragen	2 2 39,c)
cash desk	Kasse	**Add 6** 114,12
castle	Burg	**Add 7** 116,3
cat	Katze	FS 8 24,1
chair	Stuhl	FS 7 20,a)
cheese	Käse	7 2 95,3
child	Kind	4 1 59,2
⟨**children**	Kinder	3 *Photo page* 46⟩
children	Kinder	4 1 58
°**chips**	Pommes frites	FP 2 103,3
chocolate	Schokolade	6 2 83
°**church**	Kirche	5 4 77,4
°**circus**	Zirkus	FP 1 100,1
⟨to **clap**	klatschen	7 3 99,8⟩
class	Klasse	4 3 67,8
clean	sauber	FS 7 20,a)
to clean	reinigen	2 2 39,c)
to **climb**	klettern	3 3 51,d)
clock	Uhr	**Add 6** 110,1
ten o'clock	zehn Uhr	2 3 40,a)
clothes	Kleider	4 3 63,b)
clown	Clown	**Add 5** 109,7
coat	Mantel	4 3 63,c)
coffee	Kaffee	7 2 95,3
°**coin**	Münze	FP 3 105,5
cold		
blue with cold	blau vor Kälte	6 3 86,e)
cold	kalt	6 3 87,3
to **collect**	abholen	4 2 60
⟨school colours	Schulfarben	3 *Photo page* 46⟩

Alphabetical Word List

school colours	Schulfarben	3 1 47
What colour is/are …	Welche Farbe hat/haben …	3 1 48,2
to **come**	kommen	2 4 42
to come down	herunterkommen	3 3 52,e)
to come in	hereinkommen, *hier:* sich melden, (Funksprache)	4 2 60
Come on.	Los! Komm schon!	FS 7 21,c)
to come out	herauskommen	5 2 70,a)
to come upstairs	nach oben kommen	4 3 64,f)
comic	Comic	1 2 32,3
°**comprehension**	Textverständnis	3 1 47,1
⟨comprehensive school	Gesamtschule	3 *Photo page* 46⟩
°**comprehensive school**	Gesamtschule	3 2 49,a)
⟨cornflakes	Cornflakes	5 *Photo page* 68⟩
cornflakes	Cornflakes	Add 5 109,8 7 2 95,3
°**counter**	°Spielmarke	7 3 96
°**cousin**	Cousin, Cousine	FP 2 102,1
of **course**	natürlich	7 3 96
to **cry**	weinen	6 1 81,c)
a **cup** of tea	eine Tasse Tee	7 2 95,3
cupboard	Schrank	FS 7 20,a)
to **cut**	schneiden	6 2 84,3

D

dad	Papa, Vati	4 2 60
to **dance**	tanzen	4 1 58
°**Danish**	dänisch	1 2 32,3
dark	dunkel	3 3 52,e)
day	Tag	5 2 71,b)
the next day	am nächsten Tag	5 2 71,b)
°Oh **dear!**	Oje! Ach du meine Güte!	FS 7 21,c)
⟨detached house	Einzelhaus	7 *Photo page* 91⟩
°**dialogue**	Dialog, Gespräch	FS 1 8
°**dice**	Würfel	7 3 96
different	verschieden	6 1 81,b)
difficult	schwierig	3 2 49,d)
dining-room	Eßzimmer	7 2 95,4
dirty	schmutzig	FS 7 20,a)
to **do**	tun, machen	2 2 39,c)
to do homework	Hausaufgaben machen	3 2 49,a)
does		Add 6 112,6 7 3 96
doesn't		7 3 96
don't		7 1 92
dog	Hund	FS 9 27,2
door	Tür	FS 7 20,a)
back door	Hintertür	7 3 96
front door	Eingangstür	7 3 96
next door	nebenan	FS 8 23,c)
doorstep	Stufe vor der Tür	Add 7 117,3
°**double oh**	null null	2 1 37,2
down		
to come down	herunterkommen	3 3 52,e)
to fall down	herunterfallen	5 3 73
to put down	hinstellen	Add 5 109,7
to sit down	sich setzen	Add 5 109,7 7 3 96
°to write down	aufschreiben	FP 3 105,4
downstairs	unten nach unten	4 3 63,d)
°**dress**	Kleid	4 3 63,c)
to **drink**	trinken	7 3 97,G
to **drive**	fahren	2 2 39,a)
taxi **driver**	Taxifahrer, -in	FS 8 23,c)
°**dry**	trocken	FP 3 104,2
duck	Ente	4 1 58

E

early	früh	5 2 70,a)
	zu früh	Add 6 111,4
easy	leicht	3 2 49,d)
to **eat**	essen	7 1 92
⟨egg	Ei	5 *Photo page* 68⟩
egg	Ei	7 2 95,3
eight	acht	2 1 37
eighteen	achtzehn	5 1 69
°**elephant**	Elefant	FP 1 100,1
eleven	elf	2 1 37
empty	leer	FS 8 23,c)
°**end**	Ende	FP 3 105,5
to end	enden	7 3 96
English	englisch	FS 3 10,b)
in English	auf englisch	1 2 31,a)
evening	Abend	FS 9 26,a)
every	jeder, jede, jedes	5 2 70,a)
everbody	jeder	6 1 81,b)
everyone	jeder(mann), alle	7 3 96
exact	genau	Add 6 110,1
°**example**	Beispiel	FS 4 13,4
for example	zum Beispiel	5 4 75
°**exciting**	aufregend	3 3 51,c)
exercise	Übung	3 2 49,c)
exercise book	Heft	3 2 49,c)
Take an °**extra** turn.	*hier:* Du darfst noch einmal würfeln.	7 3 96

F

face	Gesicht	5 4 75
to **fall**		
to fall down	herunterfallen	5 3 73
to fall over a stone	über einen Stein fallen	6 3 85,c)

Alphabetical Word List

family	Familie	1 2 32,3
far	weit	Add 7 117,3
°farm	Bauernhof	FP 2 102,1
father	Vater	FS 5 14,b)
⟨feet	Füße	7 3 99,8
felt pen	Filzstift	1 3 33,b)
to fetch	holen	Add 5 109,9
fifteen	fünfzehn	5 1 69
to find	finden	FS 4 12,2
⟨finger	Finger	7 3 99,8
°finger	Finger	FP 3 105,5
first	der, die, das erste, die ersten	FS 1 7
	zuerst	1 3 33,a)
five	fünf	2 1 37
flat	Wohnung	FS 5 14,a)
floor	Fußboden	FS 7 20,a)
to fly	fliegen	5 3 73
	fliegen lassen	6 1 81,a)
food	Essen, Nahrung	6 2 83
football	Fußball	4 1 58
for	für	1 1 29,a)
°for a week	eine Woche (lang)	FP 2 102,1
for an answer	als Antwort	7 1 92
⟨for breakfast	zum Frühstück	5 *Photo page* 68⟩
for breakfast	zum Frühstück	7 2 95,3
for example	zum Beispiel	5 4 75
to look for	suchen	3 3 52,h)
to wait for	warten auf	2 4 44,G
to forget	vergessen	Add 7 116,3
°form	Form	1 1 30,2
four	vier	2 1 37
fourteen	vierzehn	5 1 69
Friday	Freitag	5 4 78,5
friend	Freund	FS 5 14,1
from	von, aus	FS 4 11,d)
love from	viele liebe Grüße von	Add 5 109,8
where … from	woher	FS 4 11,d)
front door	Eingangstür	7 3 96
in **front** of the shop	vor dem Laden	FS 7 21,c)
full	voll	3 2 49,c)
°fun	Spaß	FP 1 100
funny	lustig	2 3 40,b)

G

game	Spiel	2 1 38,6
⟨gay	fröhlich	6 3 89,8⟩
German	deutsch	1 1 29,b)
to get		
to get into	einsteigen	6 3 85,b)
to get lost	sich verirren, sich verlaufen	5 4 75
to get off	aussteigen	Add 7 116,3
to get out	herauskommen	3 3 52,f)
to get to	zur Leeds Road	5 1 69,1
	kommen/ gelangen	
to get up	aufstehen	5 2 70,a)
girl	Mädchen	FS 3 10,a)
to give	geben	4 3 65,2
glass	Glas	6 2 83
to go		
to go for a walk	spazierengehen	2 2 39,d)
to go on	weitermachen	FS 9 27,2
to go out	weggehen	4 3 63,a)
to go to bed	ins Bett gehen	7 3 96
to go to the seaside	ans Meer fahren	6 1 81,a)
°all **gone**	alles weg	6 2 83,b)
Timmy is gone.	Timmy is verschwunden.	Add 7 117,3
Five questions gone.	Fünf Fragen weg.	7 1 92
good	gut	FS 1 8
Have a good time.	Viel Spaß!	Add 7 116,3
goodbye	auf Wiedersehen	4 3 63,a)
has/have **got**	haben, besitzen	FS 7 20,b)
great	prima, großartig	FS 8 23,b)
green	grün	3 1 47
grey	grau	3 1 47
°group	Gruppe	FP 3 104,1
°to **guess**	raten	7 1 92

H

half past (eight)	halb (neun)	5 2 70,a)
hall	Flur	7 3 96
°handle	Klinke, Türgriff	3 3 51,b)
Hands up!	Hände hoch!	7 1 92
to happen	geschehen, passieren	Add 5 106,3 6 3 86,e)
happy	glücklich	Add 5 108,6 6 1 81,b)
⟨harbour	Hafen	6 *Photo page* 80⟩
hat	Hut	4 3 63,c)
to have		
he has got	er hat	FS 7 20,b)
she hasn't got	sie hat nicht	FS 7 20,b)
they have got	sie haben, besitzen	FS 8 23,a)
they haven't got	sie haben nicht, besitzen nicht	FS 8 24,1
to have a bath	ein Bad nehmen	7 3 96
to have a good time	viel Spaß haben	Add 7 116,3
Have a piece …	Nimm ein Stück …	6 2 83,b)
to have breakfast	frühstücken	5 4 75
to have for breakfast	zum Frühstück essen	7 2 95,3
⟨I've got it.	Verstanden.	4 2 60,4⟩
to have got on	anhaben	4 3 63,c)
he	er	FS 3 10,a)
he's	er ist	FS 4 11,c)

one hundred and seventy-one

Alphabetical Word List

he's got	er hat	4 3 67,7
head	Kopf	4 3 64,f)
to **hear**	hören	4 2 60
hello	hallo	FS 1 8,b)
to **help**	helfen	2 2 39
hen	Huhn	4 1 58
her	ihr	FS 3 10,b)
her (= Obj. Pron.)	sie, ihr	4 2 60
here	hier	FS 4 11,b)
	hierher	3 3 51,d)
here's	hier ist	1 1 30,G
here you are	Bitteschön.	6 2 84,2
high	hoch	3 3 52,f)
him	ihn, ihm	4 2 60
⟨hip, hip, hooray⟩	hip hip hurra	6 3 89,8⟩
his	sein	FS 3 10,a)
°**hobby**	Hobby	FP 2 103,2
to **hold**	halten	5 3 73
to hold a jumble sale	einen Flohmarkt abhalten (für Wohltätigkeitszwecke)	5 2 71,b)
°**hole**	Loch	5 3 73
⟨**holiday**	Ferien	6 3 89,8⟩
on **holiday**	in den Ferien	FP 2 102,1
home		
at home	zu Hause	FS 9 26,a)
to take home	nach Hause bringen	5 2 70,a)
homework	Hausaufgaben	3 2 49
to do homework	Hausaufgaben machen	3 2 49,a)
Hooray!	Hurra!	7 1 92
°**hopscotch**	Himmel und Hölle, Huckekasten	2 3 40,a)
horse	Pferd	4 1 58
hotel	Hotel	4 2 60
hour	Stunde	6 3 86,e)
house	Haus	FS 5 14,a)
how		
how many	wie viele	2 1 38,4
how old	wie alt	2 1 37,1
hungry	hungrig	6 2 83,b)

I

I	ich	FS 1 8,a)
I am	ich bin	FS 4 12,2
I'm	ich bin	FS 1 8,a)
I'm sorry.	Tut mir leid.	FS 4 11,c)
I've got	ich habe	4 2 60
idea	Idee, Vorstellung	FS 3 10
no idea	keine Ahnung	FS 3 10
⟨**if**	wenn, falls	7 3 99,8⟩
if	ob	Add 7 115,1
ill	krank	FS 4 11,b)
in	in	FS 2 9,b)
in English	auf englisch	1 2 31,a)
in front of	vor	FS 7 21,c)
in the morning	morgens	FS 9 26,a)
to come in	hereinkommen, hier: sich melden (Funksprache)	4 2 60
to look in	hineinschauen	3 3 51,c)
interesting	interessant	Add 7 116,3
into the shop	in den Laden (hinein)	2 3 40,b)
is	ist	FS 1 8,a)
she isn't	sie ist nicht	FS 6 17,a)
it	es	FS 4 11,b)
it's	es ist	FS 4 11,b)
its name	hier: sein Name	5 4 79,8

J

jacket	Jacke, Jackett	4 3 63,c)
jeans	Jeans	3 1 47
job	Job, Arbeit	5 2 70
°**joke**	Spaß	FP 3 104
°**jumble** sale	Flohmarkt (für Wohltätigkeitszwecke)	5 2 71,b)
to **jump**	springen	Add 5 108,6
		FP 2 103,3
just		
just a minute	einen Augenblick	4 2 60
just now	gerade jetzt	4 2 60
just when I'm winning	gerade jetzt, wo ich gewinne	7 1 92

K

key	Schlüssel hier: Taste	Add 5 108,6
°to **kick**	treten	3 3 52,g)
kitchen	Küche	Add 5 108,6
		7 2 95,4
kite	Drachen	5 3 73
to **know**	wissen	7 1 93,2

L

°**lady**	Dame	4 1 59,2
at **last**	endlich	Add 7 116
he is **late**	er hat sich verspätet	FS 4 11,c)
later	später	6 3 86,e)
to **laugh**	lachen	6 3 85,b)
to laugh at	auslachen	6 3 85,b)
to **leave**	verlassen	Add 5 109,8
	abfahren	Add 6 111,3
left		
on the left	auf der linken Seite	3 3 51,b)
lemonade	Limonade	6 2 83
piano **lesson**	Klavierstunde	Add 5 108,6
⟨**let's** ...	laßt uns ...	FS 9 27,4⟩
let's ...	laßt uns ...	1 3 33

Alphabetical Word List

letter	Brief	**Add 5** 109,8 6 1 82,3	
°**lid**	Deckel	**FP 3** 105,5	
light	Licht	**Add 5** 108,6	
to **like**	lieben, mögen	5 4 76	
What's the weather like?	Wie ist das Wetter?	6 3 89,7	
to **listen**	zuhören	**FS 2** 9	
⟨**little**	klein	4 3 67,10⟩	
little Jane	die kleine Jane	**Add 5** 108,6	
to **live**	leben	**Add 6** 113,11 7 3 99,6	
to **lock**	verschließen	**Add 5** 109,7	
long	lang	1 1 30,2	
to **look**	schauen	**FS 2** 9	
to look after someone	auf jemanden aufpassen	6 1 81,c)	
to look at	anschauen	**FS 3** 10,a)	
°to look brown	braun aussehen	**FP 3** 104,2	
to look for	suchen	3 3 52,h)	
to look in	hineinschauen	3 3 51,c)	
to look out of	hinausschauen	**Add 7** 116,3	
to look unhappy	unglücklich aussehen	**Add 7** 117,3	
to get **lost**	sich verlaufen, sich verirren	5 4 75	
a **lot** of	viel(e)	3 1 47	
love from	viele liebe Grüße von	**Add 5** 109,8	
°**lovely**	schön	**FP 2** 103,3	
bad **luck**	Pech	7 3 96	
°**lucky**			
°you're lucky	du hast Glück	1 2 31,a)	
lunch	Mittagessen	5 4 75	

M

magazine	Zeitschrift	1 2 32,3
°**magic**	Zauberei	**FP 3** 104
to **make**	machen	**FS 4** 13,4
man	Mann	**FS 6** 17,b)
how **many** …	wie viele …	2 1 38,4
map	Karte	1 3 33,c)
⟨**marmalade**	Marmelade	5 *Photo page* 68⟩
marmalade	Marmelade	7 2 95,3
°**matchbox**	Streichholzschachtel	**FP 3** 105,5
What's the **matter**?	Was ist los?	6 1 81,c)
me	mir, mich	2 2 39,a)
to **mean**	bedeuten	7 3 96
men	Männer	4 1 58
°What a **mess**!	Was für ein Durcheinander!	**FP 1** 101,2
milk	Milch	**Add 5** 109,8 6 2 83
milkman	Milchmann	**Add 5** 109,8
to **mind**		
I don't mind.	Es ist mir egal!	**Add 7** 115,2
Never mind.	Macht nichts!	4 3 63,b)
minute	Minute	4 2 60
Just a minute.	Einen Augenblick!	4 2 60
Wait a minute.	Augenblick mal!	6 1 82,3
to **miss** a turn	eine Runde aussetzen	7 3 96
°**missing**	fehlend	3 1 48,4
Monday	Montag	5 2 72,5
more	noch etwas, mehr	7 2 95,5
morning	Morgen	**FS 1** 8
in the morning	morgens	**FS 9** 26,a)
on Saturday morning	am Samstag morgen	2 3 40,a)
mother	Mutter	**FS 5** 14,b)
Mr	Herr (Anrede)	**FS 5** 14,2
Mrs	Frau (Anrede)	**FS 1** 8,a)
mum	Mama, Mutti	**FS 6** 17,a)
°**museum**	Museum	6 1 81,a)
music	Musik	**Add 5** 108,6
⟨music man	Musikant	5 4 78,7⟩
must	müssen	3 1 47
they °mustn't	sie dürfen nicht	5 2 71,G
my	mein, meine	**FS 1** 8,a)
mysterious	geheimnisvoll	**Add 5** 108,6

N

name	Name	**FS 1** 8,a)
°**near**	in der Nähe	**FP 2** 103,3
°**nearly**	beinahe, fast	2 1 37,1
neighbour	Nachbar	**Add 5** 108,6
never	niemals	5 4 77,G
Never mind.	Macht nichts!	4 3 63,b)
new	neu	**FS 1** 8,b)
⟨**newsagent**	Zeitungshändler	1 *Authentic Britain,* 35⟩
newspaper	Zeitung	1 2 32,3
next	als nächstes	6 1 82,2
next door	nebenan	**FS 8** 23,c)
the next day	am nächsten Tag	5 2 71,b)
I'm next.	Ich bin der/die nächste.	1 3 33,a)
nice	nett, hübsch	**Add 7** 116,3
at **night**	nachts	**FS 9** 26,a)
nine	neun	2 1 37
nineteen	neunzehn	5 1 69
no	nein	**FS 2** 9,2
no idea	keine Ahnung	**FS 3** 10
nobody	niemand	4 2 60
noise	Lärm	**Add 5** 108,6
not	nicht	**FS 2** 9,a)
not again	nicht schon wieder	**Add 6** 112,7 7 3 96
not at all	überhaupt nicht	**Add 7** 117,3
not really	eigentlich nicht	7 1 92
not yet	noch nicht	**Add 5** 108,6
now	jetzt	**FS 7** 21,c)
just now	gerade jetzt	4 2 60
number	Nummer	2 1 37,2

Alphabetical Word List

O

⟨ocean	Ozean	2 4 44,6⟩
10 **o'clock**	10 Uhr	2 3 40,a）
of		
of course	natürlich, sicher	7 3 96
to be afraid of	Angst haben vor	4 3 64,f）
in front of the shop	vor dem Laden	FS 7 21,c）
a lot of	viel, viele	3 1 47
to think of something	an etwas denken	7 1 92
⟨**often**	oft	5 *Photo page* 68⟩
often	oft	5 2 70,a）
°**oh**	oh	FS 2 9,a）
	null	2 1 37,2
°Oh dear!	Oje!	FS 7 21,c）
O.K.	In Ordnung!	1 3 33,a）
old	alt	2 1 37,1
on	auf	FS 5 14,b）
Come on.	Los! Gehen wir!	FS 7 21,c）
to go on	fortfahren	FS 9 27,2
to have got on	tragen, anhaben	4 3 63,b）
to put on	anziehen	6 3 86,e）
on holiday	in den Ferien	FP 2 102,1
on Saturday morning	am Samstag vormittag	2 3 40,a）
on the left	auf der linken Seite, links	3 3 51,b）
on the right	auf der rechten Seite, rechts	3 3 51,b）
on time	pünktlich	Add 6 110,1
one	eins	1 1 37
°1 A (one A)	Eins A	FS 3 10,a）
°1 B (one B)	Eins B	FS 2 9,b）
only	nur	3 3 51,b）
the only way	der einzige Weg	Add 7 117,3
onto the floor	auf den Boden	4 3 64,f）
to **open**	öffnen	3 3 51,b）
open	offen, auf	3 3 52,h）
°**opposite**	Gegenteil, Gegensatz	3 3 55,7
or	oder	FS 5 14,2
orange	Apfelsine	6 2 83
°**order**	Reihenfolge	FP 2 103,3
°to put in the right **order**	in die richtige Reihenfolge bringen	FP 2 103,3
other	der/die/das andere	5 4 76
our	unser, unsere	FS 5 14,b）
out	draußen, nicht zu Hause	FS 9 26,a）
to come out	herauskommen	5 2 70,a）
to get out	herauskommen	3 3 52,f）
to get out of	aussteigen, herkommen	6 3 85,c）
to go out	weggehen	4 3 63,a）
to take out	herausnehmen	4 3 63,b）
Over and out.	Ende der Durchsage! *(Funksprache)*	4 2 60
outside	draußen	7 3 98,5
Over to you.	Du bist/Ihr seid/ Sie sind dran.	FS 1 8,4
°**over**	vorbei	FP 2 102,1
over	Ende *(Funksprache)*	4 2 60
Over and out.	Ende der Durchsage! *(Funksprache)*	4 2 60
over there	dort drüben	1 3 33,c）
over the wall	über die Mauer	5 4 75
to fall over a stone	über einen Stein fallen	6 3 85,c）

P

packet	Packung, Schachtel	6 2 83
page	Seite	2 3 41,3
°**paper**	Papier	FP 3 104,2
°a piece of paper	ein Blatt Papier	FP 3 104,2
parents	Eltern	FS 8 23,a）
park	Park	5 3 73
°**party**	Party	FP 3 105,4
passenger	Passagier, Fahrgast	4 2 60
half **past** seven	halb acht	5 2 70
pen	Füller	1 3 33,b）
felt pen	Filzstift	1 3 33,b）
pencil	Bleistift	1 3 33,b）
pencil case	Federmappe	1 3 33,c）
people	Leute	4 3 63,d）
perhaps	vielleicht	4 2 60
pet	Haustier, Liebling	5 4 75
photo	Foto	6 3 87,2
⟨photo page	Fotoseite	2 36⟩
piano lesson	Klavierstunde	Add 5 108,6
piano player	Klavierspieler	Add 5 108,6
to **pick** up	aufheben	5 3 73
picnic	Picknick	6 1 81,a）
picture	Bild	2 3 41,3
picture-book	Bilderbuch	4 1 59,1
piece	Teil, Stück	4 1 58
°a piece of paper	ein Blatt Papier	FP 3 104,2
water-**pistol**	Wasserpistole	FS 7 21,c）
plan	Plan, Vorhaben	6 1 81,a）
plastic	Plastik	6 2 84,3
⟨**play**	Spiel	2 *Photo page* 36⟩
to **play**	spielen	1 3 33,a）
°**playtime**	Pause	6 3 88,G
⟨role play	Rollenspiel	4 2 62,4）
role **play**	Rollenspiel	6 2 84,2
piano **player**	Klavierspieler	Add 5 108,6
please	bitte	FS 4 11,d）
°**police**	Polizei	2 1 37,2

Alphabetical Word List

poor	arm	6 3 85,a)
°potty	Töpfchen	2 4 42
pound (£)	Pfund *(englische Währung)*	2 1 38,4
to pull	ziehen	3 3 52,f)
pullover	Pullover	2 2 39,d)
to push	schieben	3 3 52,f)
to put	stellen	3 3 51,d)
to put down	hinstellen	Add 5 109,7
to put on	anziehen	6 3 86,e)
°to put in the right order	in die richtige Reihenfolge bringen	FP 2 103,3
°puzzle	Puzzle	4 1 58

Q

quarter to	viertel vor	5 2 70,a)
question	Frage	FS 4 12,1

R

°rabbit	Kaninchen	FP 3 105,6
radio	Radio	4 2 60
by radio	per Funk	4 2 60
°railway	Eisenbahn	6 1 81,a)
to rain	regnen	2 3 40,b)
to read	lesen	1 2 31,b)
ready	fertig	6 2 84,3
not really	eigentlich nicht	7 1 92
⟨red	rot	3 *Photo page* 46⟩
red	rot	3 1 47
register	Klassenbuch	FS 4 11,b)
°to remember	sich erinnern	FP 3 105,4
°reporter	Reporter	5 2 70
°request	(Platten-) Wunsch	6 3 86,f)
to ride	reiten	4 1 58
to ride away on a bike	mit einem Fahrrad wegfahren	5 4 75
right	richtig	FS 4 12,2
right	rechts	3 3 51,b)
on the right	auf der rechten Seite, rechts	3 3 51,b)
to ring up	anrufen	Add 7 117,3
river	Fluß	Add 7 117,3
road	Straße	FS 5 14
⟨role-play	Rollenspiel	4 2 62,4⟩
role-play	Rollenspiel	6 2 84,2
roll	Brötchen	7 2 95,3
room	Zimmer	2 4 42
°round York	in York herum	FP 2 102,1
round the house	um das Haus herum	Add 7 117,3
rubber	Radiergummi	1 3 33,b)
ruler	Lineal	1 3 33,b)
to run	laufen	2 2 39,b)
to run after	hinterherrennen	5 3 73
to run away	weglaufen	5 3 73

S

jumble sale	Flohmarkt	5 2 71,b)
⟨sands	Sandstrand	6 *Photo page* 80⟩
sandwich	belegtes Brot	6 2 83
Saturday	Samstag	2 3 40
⟨sausage	Würstchen	5 *Photo page* 68⟩
sausage	Wurst	7 2 95,3
to say	sprechen, sagen	FS 2 9
°scenes	Szenen	FS 1 7
at school	in der Schule	FS 9 26,a)
school-bag	Schulranzen	1 3 33,c)
⟨school colours	Schulfarben	3 *Photo page* 46⟩
school colours	Schulfarben	3 1 47
school °uniform	Schuluniform	3 1 47
⟨Comprehensive School	Gesamtschule	3 *Photo page* 46⟩
Comprehensive School	Gesamtschule	3 2 49,a)
⟨sea	Meer	2 4 44,6⟩
sea	Meer	6 3 85,c)
to the seaside	an das Meer	6 1 81,a)
seat	Sitz	Add 7 116,3
second	der/die/das zweite	Add 5 109,9
°secret	Geheimnis	3 3 56
	geheim	FP 3 104,2
to see	sehen	3 2 49,d)
self service	Selbstbedienung	Add 6 114,12
to sell	verkaufen	7 1 92
⟨semi-detached house	Doppelhaushälfte	7 *Photo page* 91⟩
to send	schicken	4 2 60
°sentence	Satz	2 2 39,1
seven	sieben	2 1 37
seventeen	siebzehn	5 1 69
she	sie	FS 3 10,b)
she's	sie ist	FS 4 11,b)
to shine	scheinen	2 3 40,a)
shirt	Hemd	3 1 47
shoe	Schuh	3 1 47
shop	Geschäft	FS 5 14,b)
short	kurz	1 1 30,2
to shout	rufen	5 4 75
⟨to show	zeigen	7 3 99,8⟩
°to show	zeigen	Add 5 109,7
		FP 2 102,1
°to shut	schließen	FP 3 105,4
⟨sign	Zeichen	3 *Authentic page* 57⟩
silly	albern	7 3 96
⟨to sing	singen	FS 9 27,4⟩
to sing	singen	Add 6 112,7
sister	Schwester	FS 5 14,b)
to sit	sitzen	2 3 40,a)
to sit down	sich setzen	Add 5 109,7
		7 3 96

Alphabetical Word List

English	German	Ref
to sit up	sich aufrichten	4 3 64,g⟩
sitting-room	Wohnzimmer	Add 5 108,6
		7 3 96
six	sechs	2 1 37
sixteen	sechzehn	2 1 37,1
skirt	Rock	3 1 47
to **sleep**	schlafen	5 4 76
small	klein	3 3 51,d)
°**smoke**	Rauch	6 3 85,b)
snack-bar	Imbißstube	Add 6 114,12
⟨to **snap**	schnippen	7 3 99,8⟩
°**so**	also, deshalb	FS 9 26,a)
so wonderful	so großartig	Add 7 116,3
sock	Socke	3 1 47
some	einige	Add 6 112,7
		FP 2 103,2
somebody	(irgend) jemand	6 3 86,f)
someone	jemand	4 3 64,e)
sometimes	manchmal	FS 9 26,a)
⟨**song**	Lied	FS 9 27,4⟩
song	Lied	Add 6 112,7
°**soon**	bald	FP 3 104,2
Sorry.	Entschuldigung!	FS 2 9,a)
	Tut mir leid.	
I'm sorry.	Es tut mir leid.	FS 4 11,c)
to **speak**	sprechen	1 2 31
°**special**	hier: Sonder-	6 3 85
	sendung	
°to **spell**	buchstabieren	3 3 56
sponge	Schwamm	FS 7 20,b)
Ssh!	Sch(t)! Psst!	4 3 64,e)
stairs	Treppenstufen	3 3 51,c)
⟨to **stamp**	stampfen	7 3 99,8⟩
to **stand**	stehen	3 3 51,d)
to **start**	anfangen	5 2 70,a)
station	Bahnhof	4 2 60
bus station	Busbahnhof	6 3 85,b)
°to **stay**	bleiben	FP 2 102,1
step	Schritt, Stufe	1 1 29
stick	Stock	5 3 73
°**still**	noch	2 1 37,1
stone	Stein	6 3 85,c)
bus **stop**	Bushaltestelle	Add 7 116,3
to **stop**	anhalten	Add 7 116,3
story	Geschichte	4 2 62,2
street	Straße	Add 7 116,3
string	Schnur	5 3 73
suddenly	plötzlich	Add 5 108,6
sun	Sonne	2 3 40,a)
Sunday	Sonntag	5 2 71,G
⟨**surely**	sicherlich	7 3 99,8⟩
sweets	Süßigkeiten	6 2 83
sweet shop	Süßwarenladen	Add 7 116,3
to **swim**	schwimmen	4 1 58
to **switch on/off**	ein-, ausschalten	Add 5 108,6

T

English	German	Ref
table	Tisch	2 1 38,5
to **take** to	bringen	4 2 60
°to take an extra turn	hier: noch einmal würfeln	7 3 96
to take home	nach Hause bringen	5 2 70,a)
to take off	ausziehen	Add 6 112,6
to take out	herausnehmen	4 3 63,b)
to take to bed	ins Bett bringen	5 4 76
to **talk** to	sprechen (mit)	4 2 60
taxi	Taxi	FS 7 22,8
taxi-driver	Taxifahrer(in)	FS 8 23,c)
tea	Tee	5 4 76
a cup of tea	eine Tasse Tee	7 2 95,3
to **teach**	beibringen, unterrichten, lehren	5 3 73
teacher	Lehrer/-in	FS 1 8,a)
°**teddy**	Teddy(bär)	FS 9 27,2
telephone	Telefon	FS 9 26,b)
to telephone	telefonieren	4 2 60
⟨to **tell**	erzählen	4 3 67,9⟩
to **tell**	erzählen	Add 5 107,4
		6 1 81,b)
ten	zehn	2 1 37
⟨**terraced house**	Reihenhaus	7 Photo page 91⟩
terrible	fürchterlich, hier: unmöglich	FS 5 14,b)
°to **test**	prüfen, abfragen	1 3 33
°**textbook**	Schulbuch	3 2 49,b)
Thank you.	Danke!	FS 2 9,b)
Thanks.	Danke!	3 2 49,b)
No, thanks.	Nein danke!	7 1 93,3
that	das da	FS 5 14,b)
that is	das ist	FS 5 14,b)
that's	das ist	1 1 29,a)
that boy	dieser Junge	FS 3 10,a)
that's why	deshalb	7 3 96
the	der/die/das	FS 3 10,b)
their (van)	ihr (Liefer-wagen)	FS 6 17,b)
them	sie, ihnen	4 2 60
then	dann	1 3 33,a)
O.K. then.	Also, dann in Ordnung.	4 3 63,a)
there is	da ist	FS 8 23,c)
there's	da ist	1 1 29,a)
there	dorthin	4 2 62,4
over there	dort drüben	1 3 33,c)
up there	dort oben	3 3 52,h)
these	diese hier	4 1 58
they	sie	FS 6 17,b)
they are	sie sind	FS 6 17,b)
they're	sie sind	FS 6 17,b)
thing	Ding, Sache	5 2 70,a)
to **think**	denken, meinen	6 1 81,1

Alphabetical Word List

to think of something	an etwas denken	7 1 92
third	der/die/das dritte	Add 5 109,9
thirsty	durstig	6 2 83,b)
thirteen	dreizehn	5 1 69
this	dies, dieser, diese	1 3 33,b)
What's this in English?	Wie heißt dies auf englisch?	1 3 33,b)
those	diese dort	4 1 58
three	drei	2 1 37
through	(hin)durch	3 3 51,d)
to throw	werfen	4 3 64,f)
Thursday	Donnerstag	5 4 78,5
to tie	befestigen	6 2 84,3
°tights	Strumpfhose	3 1 47
time	Zeit, Uhrzeit	5 2 72,3
on time	pünktlich	Add 6 111,3
What time is it?	Wie spät ist es?	5 2 72,3
timetable	Fahrplan	Add 6 111,3
to		
Over to you.	Du bist/Ihr seid/ Sie sind dran.	FS 1 8,4
to get to school	zur Schule kommen	5 2 70,a)
quarter to	viertel vor	5 2 70,a)
to take s.o. to	jdn zu einem Ort bringen	4 2 60
to talk to	sprechen mit	4 2 60
⟨toast	Toast	5 *Photo page 68*⟩
toast	Toast	7 2 95,3
today	heute	1 1 29,a)
together	zusammen, gemeinsam	3 2 49,a)
too	auch	FS 5 14,a)
too big	zu groß	3 3 51,d)
°tourist	Tourist(in)	FP 2 102,1
town	Stadt	7 3 99,6
toy	Spielzeug	FS 9 27,3
toy telephone	Spielzeugtelefon	FS 9 26,b)
°tractor	Traktor	FP 2 103,3
train	Zug	6 1 81
by train	mit dem Zug	6 1 81
tray	Tablett	Add 6 114,12
°treasure	Schatz	3 3 52,e)
trick	Trick, Kunststück	5 3 73
trousers	Hose	3 1 47
°trunk	Rüssel	FP 1 101,2
Tuesday	Dienstag	5 4 78,5
turn		
It's Ronny's turn.	Ronny ist an der Reihe.	7 1 92
to miss a turn	eine Runde aussetzen	7 3 96
°to take an extra turn	*hier:* noch einmal würfeln	7 3 96
TV	Fernsehen	2 4 42,2
to watch TV	fernsehen	2 4 42,2
twelve	zwölf	2 1 37
twenty	zwanzig	3 2 50,4
twenty-one	einundzwanzig	5 1 69
two	zwei	FS 8 23,c)

U

Ugh!	i! i gitt!	7 3 96
°uncle	Onkel	FP 2 103,3
under	unter	FS 7 20,b)
°to understand	verstehen	FP 3 104,2
unhappy	unglücklich	6 3 85,a)
to look unhappy	unglücklich aussehen	Add 7 117,3
°uniform	Uniform	3 1 47
°unit	Einheit	1 1 28
until	bis	7 3 96
up		
up there	dort oben	3 3 52,h)
to get up	aufstehen	5 2 70,a)
Hands up!	Hände hoch!	7 1 92
to pick up	aufheben	5 3 73
to ring up	anrufen	Add 7 117,3
to sit up	sich aufrichten	4 3 64,g)
to wake someone up	jdn aufwecken	5 4 75
to wash up	abwaschen	7 3 96
upstairs	oben, nach oben	4 3 64,f)
to come upstairs	nach oben kommen	4 3 64,f)
us	uns	4 1 58
to use	benutzen, verwenden	7 1 92
useful	nützlich	7 1 92
usually	normalerweise	Add 5 109,8 7 2 95,3

V

van	Lieferwagen	FS 5 14,b)
very	sehr	4 3 63,b)
village	Dorf	5 2 70,a)
⟨violin	Violine	5 4 78,7⟩
to visit	besuchen	7 2 95,5
°vocabulary	Wortschatz	1 3 34,2
voice	Stimme	Add 7 117,3

W

to wait	warten	2 4 42
to wait for	warten auf	2 4 44,G
to wake someone up	jdn aufwecken	5 4 75
walk	Spaziergang	2 2 39,d)
to go for a walk	einen Spaziergang machen	2 2 39,d)
to walk	laufen, zu Fuß gehen	Add 6 110,2 6 3 88,4
to walk back	zurückgehen	Add 7 116,3
wall	Mauer	2 3 40,a)

one hundred and seventy-seven 177

Alphabetical Word List

over the wall	über die Mauer	5 4 75
to **want**	wollen, mögen	5 2 71,b)
warm	warm	6 3 86,e)
to **wash**	waschen	5 4 75
to wash up	abwaschen	7 3 96
watch	Armbanduhr	Add 7 117,3
to **watch**	schauen, zugucken beachten	2 3 40,a) Add 6 111,5
to watch TV	fernsehen	2 4 42,2
water	Wasser	FS 7 20,b)
water-pistol	Wasserpistole	FS 7 21,c)
on his **way** back	auf dem Rückweg	Add 7 117,3
we	wir	FS 5 14,a)
we are	wir sind	FS 5 16,4
we're	wir sind	FS 5 14,a)
to **wear**	tragen	2 2 39,d)
weather		
What's the weather like?	Wie ist das Wetter?	6 3 89,7
Wednesday	Mittwoch	5 4 78,5
week	Woche	5 4 78,5
°for a week	eine Woche lang	FP 2 102,1
Well, ...	Also, .../Nun, ...	FS 9 26,a)
Well, no.	Eigentlich nicht.	5 2 70,a)
what	was	FS 1 8,b)
what's	was ist, wie ist	1 1 29,b)
What about Ronny?	Was ist mit Ronny?	1 2 31,1
°What a mess!	Was für ein Durcheinander!	FP 1 100,2
What colour is ...?	Welche Farbe hat ...?	3 1 48,2
What is your name?	Wie heißt du?	FS 1 8,b)
What's the matter?	Was ist los?	6 1 81,c)
What's the weather like?	Wie ist das Wetter?	6 3 89,7
What time is it?	Wie spät ist es?	5 2 72,3
when	als	6 3 86,e)
	wenn	4 2 60
	wann	5 4 77,3
just when I'm winning	gerade jetzt wo ich gewinne	7 1 92

where	wo	FS 4 11,b)
where's	wo ist	1 1 29,a)
where ... from	woher	FS 4 11,d)
⟨white	weiß	3 *Photo page 46*⟩
white	weiß	3 1 47
who	wer	FS 8 23,b)
	wen	3 3 53,2
who's	wer ist	1 1 30,1
⟨the whole world	die ganze Welt	4 3 67,10⟩
why	warum	3 2 49,1
that's why	deshalb	7 3 96
to **win**	gewinnen	7 1 92
window	Fenster	FS 7 20,a)
at the window	am Fenster	1 1 29,b)
windy	windig	6 3 86,d)
°**winner**	Gewinner(in)	7 3 96
with	mit, bei	1 2 31,a)
blue with cold	blau vor Kälte	6 3 86,e)
woman	Frau	FS 6 17,c)
women	Frauen	4 1 58
so **wonderful**	so großartig	Add 7 116,3
word	Wort	FS 4 12,2
word order	Wortstellung	Add 6 111,5
⟨**work**	Arbeit	2 *Photo page 36*⟩
to **work**	arbeiten	3 2 50,4
⟨**world**	Welt	4 3 67, 10⟩
to **write**	schreiben	1 2 31,b)
°to write down	aufschreiben	FP 3 105,4
wrong	falsch	1 2 32,3

Y

yellow	gelb	3 1 47
yes	ja	FS 2 9,b)
	doch	FS 7 21,c)
not ... **yet**	noch nicht	Add 5 108,6
yoghurt	Joghurt	Add 6 114,12
you	du, ihr, Sie	FS 2 9,b)
	dir, euch, Ihnen	2 2 39,2
	dich, euch, Sie	3 2 49,d)
Over to you.	Du bist/Ihr seid dran.	FS 1 8,4
you're	du bist/ihr seid	FS 4 11,c)
your	dein, euer, Ihr	FS 1 8,a)
Talk about **yourself.**	Rede über dich.	Add 6 114,13

Boy's names

Andy [ˈændɪ] **FS 4** 13,5
Ben [ben] **FS 3** 10,1
Bernard [ˈbɜːnəd] **1 2** 32,3
Bob [bɒb] **5 3** 74,4
⟨Bonnie [ˈbɒnɪ] **2 4** 44,6⟩
Charlie [ˈtʃɑːlɪ] **1 2** 32,6
Dan [dæn] **FS 6** 19,7
David [ˈdeɪvɪd] **FS 1** 8,1

Don [dɒn] **FS 8** 25,6
Gordon [ˈgɔːdn] **1 2** 32,3
Jim [dʒɪm] **FS 1** 8,1
John [dʒɒn] **FS 1** 8,1
Ken [ken] **5 3** 74,4
Kevin [ˈkevɪn] **FS 1** 8,b)
Peter [ˈpiːtə] **5 4** 75
Ralph [rælf] **Add 5** 109,9

Ronny [ˈrɒnɪ] **FS 1** 8,b)
Sam [sæm] **FP 1** 100,1
Timmy [ˈtɪmɪ] **FS 8** 23,b)
Tom [tɒm] **FS 3** 10
Tommy [ˈtɒmɪ] **FP 3** 104,3
Tony [ˈtəʊnɪ] **FS 1** 8,1

Alphabetical Word List

Girl's names

Ann [æn] **FS 3** 10,1
Barbara ['bɑ:brə] **1 1** 29
Christine ['kristi:n] **FS 4** 11,b)
Helen ['helin] **FS 1** 8,1
Jane [dʒein] **FS 1** 8,1
Jenny ['dʒeni] **FS 1** 8,1
Kate [keit] **FS 5** 14,b)
Linda ['lində] **FP 1** 100,1
Mandy ['mændi] **5 4** 75
Penny ['peni] **FS 1** 8,1
Susan ['su:zn] **3 3** 55,8
Wendy ['wendi] **2 3** 41,4

Surnames

Baker [beikə] **Add 5** 109,9
Barker ['bɑ:kə] **Add 5** 109,9
Barnes [bɑ:nz] **FS 4** 11,b)
Bennett ['benit] **FS 1** 8,b)
Brown [braun] **FS 6** 17,b)
Carson ['kɑ:sən] **Add 5** 108,6
Clean [kli:n] **1 2** 32,3
Cook [kuk] **FS 4** 11,b)
Gossip ['gɒsip] **1 2** 32,3
Griffin ['grifin] **FS 1** 8,a)
Jackson ['dʒæksən] **Add 6** 110,2
MacDonald [mək'dɒnəld] **FS 4** 11,c)
Miller ['milə] **FS 6** 18,4
Morton ['mɔ:tn] **4 2** 60
Parker ['pɑ:kə] **Add 5** 109,9
Pearson ['piəsn] **FS 2** 9,b)
Stone ['stəun] **FP 1** 100,1
Webb [web] **5 2** 70
Wilson ['wilsn] **5 4** 75

Place names

Britain ['britn] **3 1** 47
Cologne [kə'ləun] **1 2** 31,a)
Denmark ['denmɑ:k] **1 1** 29,a)
Escrick ['eskrik] **5 2** 70
Fulford ['fulfəd] **1 1** 30,2
Germany ['dʒə:məni] **1 1** 29,a)
Goathland ['gəuθlənd] **Add 6** 111,3
Grosmont ['grəusmənt] **Add 6** 111,3
Heslington ['hezliŋtən] **Add 7** 115,1
Kenton ['kentən] **Add 7** 118,6
Leeds [li:dz] **FS 4** 11,d)
Levisham ['levifæm] **Add 6** 111,3
Micklegate ['miklgeit] **4 2** 60
Newcastle ['nju:kɑ:sl] **Add 7** 118,6
Pickering ['pikəriŋ] **6 1** 81,b)
Scarborough ['skɑ:bərə] **Add 6** 113,11
Scotland ['skɒtlənd] **FP 2** 102,1
Selby (Road) ['selbi] **FS 5** 14
Stillingfleet ['stiliŋfli:t] **5 2** 70
Tadcaster ['tædkæstə] **4 2** 60
Wheldrake ['weldreik] **5 2** 70
⟨Whitby ['witbi] **6** *Photo page* 80⟩
Whitby ['witbi] **6 1** 81
York [jɔ:k] **FS 1** 7

Other names

Alpha ['ælfə] **3 3** 56
BBC [,bi: bi: 'si:] **6 3** 86,e)
Bonzo ['bɒnzəu] **5 4** 75
Puddles ['pʌdlz] **Add 5** 108,6
Tangram ['tæŋgræm] **4 1** 58

Bildquellen:
Barnaby's London, p. 80 (4)
J. Allan Cash, p. 91 (1)
Jon Mather, Calverley, p. 46 (2)
Methuen, London, p. 79 (cartoons from *Top Dog* by Norman Thelwell)
Moorsrail, Pickering, p. 81, p. 90
Picturepoint, London, p. 80 (1, 2, 3), p. 91 (3)
Derek Thrippleton, York, p. 46 (1, 3), p. 57, p. 61, p. 68, p. 91 (2), p. 116
Marji Talbot, London, cover, p. 35, p. 36

Textquellen
The sun has got his hat on, p. 89 © 1932
Reproduced by permission of West's Limited
138–40 Charing Cross Road, London
WC2H OLD

⟨Useful phrases in class⟩

● **What you can say to your friends or to the teacher**

- Good morning, Mr/Mrs/Miss ... Guten Morgen ...
  Good-bye. Auf Wiedersehen.
  Thanks. Thank you (very much). Danke. Vielen Dank.

- I'm sorry. Tut mir leid.
  I'm sorry I'm late. Tut mir leid, daß ich mich verspätet habe.
  I'm not feeling well. Ich fühle mich nicht gut.
  Can I open the window? Darf ich das Fenster aufmachen?

- What's this in English/German? Was heißt dies auf englisch/deutsch?
  Can I say: ...? Kann ich sagen: ...?
  What does ... mean? Was bedeutet ...?

- Can I ask a question, please? Kann ich bitte eine Frage stellen?
  How do you do this exercise? Wie macht man/geht diese Übung?
  Can you help me, please? Können Sie/Kannst du mir bitte helfen?
  This question is difficult. Diese Frage ist schwierig.
  I don't know the answer. Ich weiß die Antwort nicht.
  Is this right? Ist das richtig?
  I don't think this is right/wrong. Ich glaube nicht, daß dies richtig/falsch ist.
  Can you repeat the question/sentence? Können Sie/Kannst du die Frage/den Satz wiederholen?

  I don't understand this word/sentence. Ich verstehe dieses Wort/diesen Satz nicht.
  Pardon? Wie bitte?
  Can you write it on the board? Können Sie es an die Tafel schreiben?

- Can we read this story? Können wir diese Geschichte bitte lesen?
  Let's act the story. Wir möchten die Geschichte spielen.
  Can we sing a song? Können wir ein Lied singen?

- What must we do for homework? Was haben wir als Hausaufgabe auf?

● **What the teacher may say to you**

- Open your books at page ... Öffnet eure Bücher auf Seite ...
  Turn to page ... Schlagt Seite ... auf.
  Read the text on page ... Lies den Text auf Seite ...
  Look at the picture on page ... Schau das Bild auf Seite ... an.

- Please fetch me some chalk. Bitte hol mir Kreide.
  Would you collect the exercise books/worksheets/workbooks? Würdest du bitte die Übungshefte/Arbeitsblätter/Arbeitsbücher einsammeln?
  Do this exercise for homework. Macht diese Übung als Hausaufgabe.
  Write the answers/sentences in your exercise book/on the board. Schreibt die Antworten in eure Übungshefte/an die Tafel.

- That's right. That's wrong. Das ist richtig. Das ist falsch.
  Good. Very good. That's good. Gut! Sehr gut! Das ist gut.
  That's not very good. Try again. Das ist nicht sehr gut. Versuch es noch einmal.
  That's better. Well done. Das ist besser. Gut gemacht.

- Be quiet. Seid ruhig.
  Sit down, please. Setzt euch bitte.
  Please speak up. Sprich lauter bitte.